the new southwest

classic flavors with a modern twist

the new southwest

classic flavors with a modern twist

by meagan micozzi of *scarletta*bakes

Hippocrene Books
New York

For more information, address:
HIPPOCRENE BOOKS, INC.
171 Madison Avenue
New York, NY 10016
www.hippocrenebooks.com

Color photographs by **Meagan Micozzi**
Book and jacket design by **Yvette Marquez-Sharpnack**
Author photograph by **Elaine Kessler**

Library of Congress Cataloging-in-Publication Data
Micozzi, Meagan.
The New Southwest : classic flavors with a modern twist / Meagan Micozzi.
    pages cm
ISBN 978-0-7818-1315-0 (hardcover) -- ISBN 0-7818-1315-8
1. Cooking, American--Southwestern style. 2. Cooking--Southwest, New. I.
Title.
 TX715.2.S69M53 2013
 641.5979--dc23
                                2013025015

Printed in the United States of America.

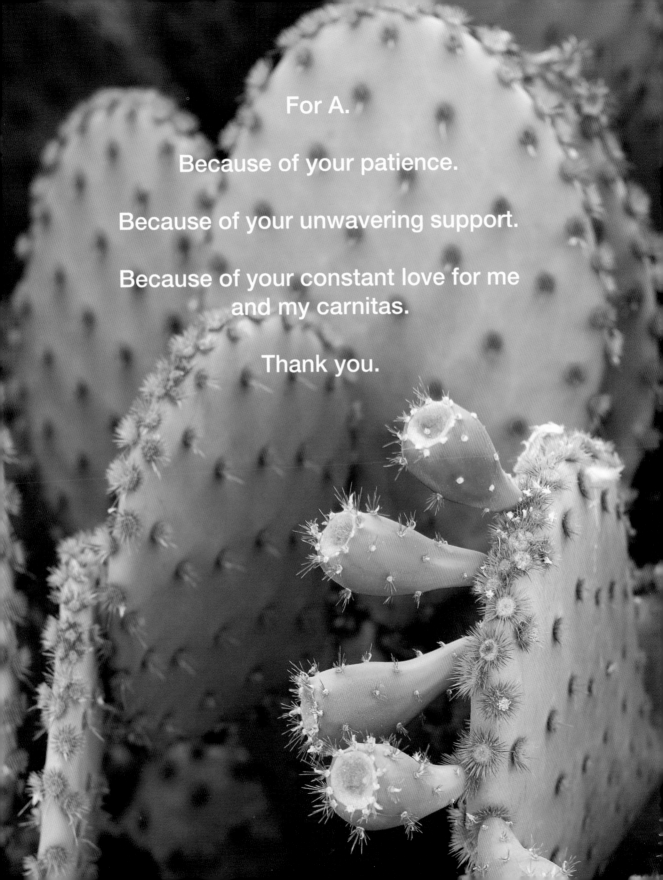

For A.

Because of your patience.

Because of your unwavering support.

Because of your constant love for me
and my carnitas.

Thank you.

contents

introduction

you find the best things in corners, don't you agree?

Whether it's the fuzzy corner of your pants pocket, the cool back corner of your refrigerator, or that delectable corner piece from a freshly-baked pan of brownies, corners seem to boast all sorts of hidden gems. Such was the case with me and that very special corner of the United States known as the American Southwest.

What first comes to mind when you think of the American Southwest? Cowboys? Cacti? Culinary options as riddled with tumbleweeds as the local desert landscape? If so, you wouldn't be too far off from what I thought before coming to make my home here.

Let's start with where you think of when you think of the Southwest. While Arizona and New Mexico form the foundation of anyone's geographic definition of the American Southwest, colloquial thinking has expanded its boundaries to include eastern Texas, southern California, and adjacent parts of Nevada, Colorado, and Utah.

The fact is that the American Southwest has not been immune to the population patterns affecting the rest of the country: mobility has expanded and eliminated boundaries, which is why most people have come to define the Southwest so much more broadly than they would have even ten years ago. For the purposes of this book, beyond just the Sonoran Desert of Arizona and the High Plains of eastern New Mexico, the Southwest now encompasses Texas Hill Country and the verdant Rio Grande Valley to the east, the grasslands of eastern Colorado and Butte Back Country in southern Utah to the north, and mountainous forestlands and desert space stretching to the coast of California in the west.

And wouldn't you know it? New spaces means new tastes, in fact, a whole new group of ingredients and culinary techniques to be exact. Which is the story of how Southwestern cuisine grew out of its cowboy boots and up into the sophisticated amalgam of flavors that it is today.

Modern Southwestern cuisine is a blend. A blend of classic desert ingredients and new, fresh additives. Think cactus paddles and agave nectar meet California avocado and seafood. Or maybe corn and beans get some Lone Star style from the flavors of chili and fresh barbecue. Perhaps Native American breads and stews bring a whole new meaning to the tacos and *tortas* that are just what people think of when they think of the Southwest. Which brings us back to my own story.

I grew up on the East Coast in a household that celebrated the cooking of classic Americana with exceptions made for nods to my German heritage. I remember meals centered around casseroles, pot pies, meatloaf, and mac & cheese. And then there was the braunschweiger … I suppose when consumed in the privacy of your own home, there is no embarrassment in the occasional meal of braunschweiger, but you try being the only girl rocking a liverwurst sandwich in a packed cafeteria on a hot summer day in Virginia. You try explaining that sandwich to your peanut butter & jelly-loving and chicken nugget-popping friends. It was enough to drive me into the warm embrace of frozen pizza and potato chips for a solid portion of my teen years.

Don't get me wrong, I always loved eating, it was just the process from the produce aisle (or in the case of my teen years, the package) to the plate that never particularly interested me. I needed something to inspire me to come back into the kitchen in a meaningful way. It just never occurred to me that I would find that catalyst in the desert of Arizona.

It may have been the fact that I knew so little and expected almost nothing when it came to finding food in my new home that initially fueled my curiosity. "Where do tacos come from?" "What goes into a burrito?" "Why are there so many chiles to pick from and what am I supposed to do with them?" There was so much to explore, and although I didn't know it at the time, I had arrived just as things were starting to get interesting.

Flash forward two years to find me smitten with the flavors of the new Southwest. I spent the better part of 2010 in front of my oven, making batch after batch of cajeta, churning out towers of fresh tortillas, and perfecting my technique for producing the perfect pan of enchiladas. When I wasn't at the stove, I was quizzing anyone who would open their kitchen to me about the best way to bake fresh Pueblo Bread, or the secret to preparing an inspired mole sauce. I would ask a question, take a taste, then go home and spend days developing my own version of so many classic Southwestern staples.

I should say that I am not a professionally trained chef. Nor am I a classically prepared pastry artist. I'm just an East Coast-raised girl who found love and a new life at the bottom of a platter of puffy tacos.

Ultimately, my style of Southwestern cuisine is a marriage of the hearty, comforting, all-American dishes that I grew up on mixed with the flavors of the Southwest. Classics like burgers and layer cakes will always have a place in my heart and my kitchen. Combine those dishes with New Mexican green chile stew, spicy carne adovada, flavorful picadillo, or warm Texas chili pie, and you've got a table that no one will want to leave.

Which is why, in so many ways, this cookbook is my love letter to the cuisine and culinary tradition of the Southwest. Because between pinto beans and pinyon nuts, chorizo and chicharrones, quinoa and quesadillas, I fell hard.

The fact of the matter is that it's easy to be passionate about modern Southwestern cuisine: this most unique melting pot of Native American, Mexican, Tex-Mex, and classic Americana has something to offer every palate. If the heat from ripe New Mexican green chiles doesn't get your blood pumping, than the warmth from a hearty Navajo taco will. Or maybe a mile-high cemita sandwich is calling your name? Perhaps a sweet slice of cake soaked in rich dulce de leche will do the trick. See? You're already swooning, too!

Because modern Southwestern cuisine is that best blend that I mentioned above. That best blend of the old and the new, of coastal flavors to the west and flamboyant flavors to the east, of hearty ranching plates to the north and fiery desert fare to the south. Modern Southwestern cuisine is one of the most inclusive that I have ever experienced. And I suppose that people like me are the reason why: bringing our experiences to the table has made its contents so much more rich and flavorful than ever before.

Scarletta Bakes the blog began as a simple electronic diary of my culinary (mis)adventures in my Arizona kitchen. As I stumbled my way through my new edible landscape, I needed a tool for documenting my successes and failures. And my progress was fueled as I began to produce more of the former than the latter, along with the fact that I absolutely loved what I was doing. My nickname, Scarletta, was given to me by my husband because of my tendency to turn fiery shades of red during indelicate moments of frustration. He would encourage red-faced Scarletta to go back into the kitchen to bake a *tres leches* cake or a pan of flan, and everyone would live happily ever after.

As the blog grew, I realized that there was still so much to be said, so much to be shared about modern Southwestern cooking. And this made sense: people were just as curious as I originally was about this desert landscape and how it could possibly produce anything of culinary value. Which is how the blog became the starting point for my take on new Southwest cooking.

For me, the new Southwest is, and will always be, a place of wide open spaces, both culinary and geographic. Ripe, buttery avocado has a hint of sweetness in it ... OK, why not put it into a sugar-glazed doughnut? Earthy, mild ancho chiles are the perfect match for warm canela ... let's bake both into a cake. This is the style of cooking (and eating) that ultimately defines the blog, this book, and ... well, me.

Looking back, I can remember reading the very first blog comment a reader ever left for me and feeling like I had just struck gold. I remember the first time someone asked me exactly what a puffy taco was. I remember a reader engaging in a lengthy discussion on the perfect technique for producing cajeta. And I remember talking chiles, chiles, and more chiles. Today, I continue to feel sincerely grateful for each and every person who pulls up a chair to share in the spicy, sweet, and savory shenanigans that I am serving up.

I truly hope that you'll enjoy cooking your way through this book; it's designed to bring a little piece of Southwestern cuisine into your kitchen and, hopefully, a smile to your face. Because I continue to believe that if you're not having fun in the kitchen, it's probably time to spice things up.

So what are you waiting for? It's time to fall in love, Southwestern-style.

the
southwestern
pantry

One of the main reasons that modern Southwestern cuisine is so exciting is that the pantry of a typical Southwestern cook has expanded to include so many foods and culinary techniques that would previously have been considered not useful or not readily available.

Nowadays, this broadened collection of ingredients, spices, and tools of the trade is more accessible than ever before, both in and outside the Southwest, which brings that many more people to the table, literally and figuratively.

Included in this chapter is a list of ingredients that I use every day in my Southwestern kitchen, as well as acceptable substitutions as applicable—while the majority of these ingredients can easily be found at large chain grocery stores across the country, I know how frustrating it is to feel excluded from preparing a dish because you simply can't find a particularly elusive item. Please note that this list is not comprehensive, but more a collection of notes on the ingredients and equipment that are most common to Southwestern cuisine, but may also be unfamiliar to anyone looking to build their own Southwestern pantry from scratch.

toasting & grinding spices: I toast and grind every single one of my spices by hand. I recognize that not everyone will have the time or inclination to adopt this practice, but when you have a moment, try dry-toasting a stick of cinnamon or a handful of cumin seeds before grinding them in a spice mill, and compare your finished product to what you get out of a jar from the shelf at your local grocery store. I guarantee you'll be both shocked and converted the minute that you do. Investing in a basic spice mill and a collection of opaque glass jars for storage, and then taking the time to toast and grind the spices that you'll be reaching for over the next few months will simply elevate your cooking to an entirely new level, whatever style of cuisine you're choosing to prepare. To dry-toast, I simply heat a comal or rimmed fry pan over a medium flame, add my spices and toast, tossing and agitating often, for 1 to 2 minutes or until spices are fragrant and just slightly turning color. Remove from heat, cool, and grind to a fine powder in a spice mill, discarding any large pieces that remain.

spices & herbs

canela: Canela is Mexican cinnamon. It's not just cinnamon that comes from Mexico or the Spanish word for cinnamon, it is actually a different type of cinnamon. Mexican cinnamon is of the Ceylon variety, while the overwhelming majority of cinnamon sold and consumed in the United States is of the Cassia variety. Cassia cinnamon originates from China and other parts of Southeast Asia. The sticks are typically rolled in a double-scroll shape and they are quite hard, requiring some muscle to grind. Ceylon cinnamon originates in Sri Lanka, is much thinner and more brittle than Cassia, and the sticks are more easily ground using a spice mill or even a mortar and pestle. Ceylon sticks are also rolled in a 'double-scroll' shape, although they are often comprised of multiple, thinner layers as opposed to Cassia's single, thick layer. You will note that most recipes in this book call for canela, with cinnamon listed as an acceptable substitute. If you have been eating canela and not cinnamon for as long as I have, you will likely agree that the taste of Cassia cinnamon is much more aggressive than that of Ceylon cinnamon from Mexico. For that reason, if you are substituting Cassia cinnamon for canela in any of the recipes listed in this book, you may wish to halve the amount that you add.

cilantro: Cilantro is one of the more divisive ingredients I have ever worked with: people seem to either love it or hate it, which is why I don't incorporate it into many dishes. Cilantro boasts an extremely herbaceous flavor often described by its detractors as astringent or 'soapy.' Although it is not an exact match in terms of taste, I usually use parsley in place of cilantro, as I find it to be much less objectionable to most guests and tablemates.

cinnamon: See Canela

coriander: Coriander is simply the dried seeds of the cilantro plant, which is why, unsurprisingly, adding dried coriander to a dish will infuse it with the distinctive, herbaceous flavor of fresh cilantro. I tend to use it sparingly, as the flavor of dried coriander is quite strong.

cumin: Cumin is one of the most ubiquitous flavors of Southwestern and Tex-Mex cuisines, one which you may recognize each time you eat a Southwestern dish, but not quite be able to identify if you don't work with it regularly. Its flavor is smoky and earthy, with just a hint of nuttiness that is enhanced by toasting the seeds. Cumin is most often thought of as an additive in chilis.

oregano: Oregano is a powerful flavor agent that I almost always use in its dried form. Note that Mexican oregano is an entirely different spice than the Mediterranean oregano that is most commonly purveyed throughout the United States. Mexican oregano is more savory and slightly stronger than its Mediterranean counterpart. While recipes in this book will call for the Mexican variety, I generally use oregano in such small amounts that you may easily substitute Mediterranean oregano if you can't find the Mexican variety in your local market.

sage: Fresh wild sage has been a part of Southwestern cooking for centuries, and remains a distinctive flavoring for meats, such as lamb and pork. The fresh leaves are delicious fried in butter, and the dried herb lends magnificent flavor to breads and bread-based dishes such as stuffing. Fresh or dried, sage should be used sparingly, as overuse will yield a medicinal flavor.

white pepper: You will note that I use ground white pepper frequently in my recipes. I do so for two reasons: first, I feel the smaller grains distribute themselves more evenly than ground black pepper in sauces, salsas, and baked goods. The second reason is purely aesthetic: I use ground white pepper because I don't want the grinds to be visible in the finished product. But in most cases, ground black pepper may be substituted if you prefer the flavor or if you don't have ground white pepper on hand.

chiles

Although they are known by different names, dried chiles are simply the desiccated version of their fresh counterparts. Ancho chiles, for example, are none other than dried poblano chile, while chipotles are dried, smoked jalapeños. Chiles, fresh or dried, are often maligned as nothing more than heat agents packing varying degrees of punch. While chiles can be spicy, each different variety boasts its own unique flavor, and should be used as such in whatever you are cooking or baking. As with my spices, I prefer to stem, seed, and toast dried chiles before working with them. For more information on preparing dried chiles, please see page 26.

dried chiles

ancho: Ancho chiles are dried poblanos and extremely mild and flavorful. They boast an earthy, slightly fruity flavor that pairs magnificently with chocolate. I will often incorporate ground ancho chiles into baked goods.

california: California chile pods, also known as *chile seco del norte*, are the dried version of Anaheim chiles. They impart an extremely mild, earthy flavor, and may be used interchangeably with dried New Mexico red chile pods, although California chiles tend to be milder than their New Mexico cousins.

chiles de árbol: These diminutive chiles pack quite a punch when it comes to heat: you'll likely only need to use a few at a time for each salsa or dish. Chiles de árbol are one of the few exceptions to the rule of different names for the fresh and dried varieties, although they are much easier to find in their dried form in markets throughout the United States. Cayenne peppers, fresh or dried, are a good substitute for chiles de árbol.

chipotle: Chipotle chiles are dried, smoked jalapeños and, as such, they lend a powerful, smoky flavor to any dish. Their skin is leathery and quite tough, which means that they take longer to toast and grind. The reward is worth the effort though, as just a bit of ground chipotle powder can add dimension and depth to anything from meat to salsas to mole sauces.

chipotle chiles in adobo sauce: These canned chipotle chiles have become a popular addition to American and Tex-Mex cooking in recent years. Dried chipotles are rehydrated in prepared adobo sauce, a smoky, heavily seasoned marinade that heightens the flavor and heat of the chipotle chiles. You can find cans of chipotle chiles in adobo sauce in the Hispanic or International section of any well-stocked grocery store.

new mexico red: Also known as *chiles de ristra* for the colorful strands on which these pods are often stored and displayed, New Mexico red chiles are an earthy, milder variety frequently used to make basic red chile or enchilada sauce (as on page 27). They are more spicy than California chiles, but less spicy than chipotle chiles.

fresh chiles

As with dried chiles, fresh chiles should not be discounted as simply purveyors of heat—each brings its own unique flavor, shape, and color to the table. When shopping for fresh chiles, seek out fruit that has a firm exterior with an almost waxy sheen; avoid chiles that are shriveled and wrinkled. It is important to note that because a significant portion of a chile's heat is carried in its seeds and membranes, removing the seeds and veins from the inside of a chile will noticeably reduce the intensity contained in each bite. Fresh chiles can simply be chopped and added directly to salsas and other dishes, but they are more frequently roasted, peeled, stemmed, seeded, and cut into flavorful strips called *rajas*. For more information on preparing fresh chiles, please see page 23.

anaheim: Anaheim chiles are typically bright green in color, long and narrow, with slight shoulders and a mild flavor. They look very similar to New Mexican Hatch chiles, but you won't want to mistake one for the other—Hatch chiles are noticeably hotter than Anaheim chiles.

habanero: Poor habanero chiles are so often maligned and eschewed as being just too hot to tolerate. Not true! They actually have a lovely, uniquely fruity flavor that makes them a wonderful additive to all kinds of stews, salsas and other dishes. Because their skin is so paper-thin, habanero chiles are not the best candidates for roasting. Instead, you can stem, seed, and chop or puree the chiles before incorporating them. While it is always necessary to take proper precaution when handling chiles, this is especially true of habaneros: I strongly recommend wearing rubber gloves and cleaning your workspace and tools thoroughly when you're done.

hatch: Hatch green chiles come from the Hatch valley of southern New Mexico and are considered to be premium green chiles. They pack an intensely flavorful and spicy punch, and often form the foundation of traditional green chili or the green chile sauce that is such an important part of New Mexican cuisine. Hatch chile season typically extends from late summer to early autumn in New Mexico.

jalapeño: Jalapeños are undoubtedly the most widely known and commonly used chile pepper in the United States; they are most often picked, sold, and consumed when they are still green, rather than when they have fully ripened to a bright shade of red. Jalapeños offer a moderate degree of heat and a fresh, slightly fruity flavor.

poblano: Incredibly versatile and wonderfully delicious whether roasted and peeled or stuffed and fried, dark green poblano chiles are the work horse of the fresh chile family. Poblanos offer an extremely mild degree of heat, and their thick flesh and large size make them extremely easy to work with.

serrano: Serrano chiles are extremely hot and should be handled with care—don't be deceived by their diminutive size. Because of their thin walls, serranos are not ideal for roasting and peeling; I prefer to boil or mince them before adding to salsas or other dishes.

produce

avocado: Fresh avocado is such a pleasure to eat and prepare and it really doesn't need much adornment at all. Ripe avocado flesh has a naturally sweet, buttery flavor that actually lends itself to more than the typical savory dishes. I will often bake with avocados, and use them in sweet breads such as the glazed doughnuts found on page 63. Due to international growing seasons, avocados can often be found in American markets year round. Ripe avocados will yield slightly when pressure is applied to their skin, and their flesh will appear green under the top stem.

green onions: I use green onions liberally as both a garnish and an ingredient in a wide variety of dishes. Note that when a recipe in this book calls for green onions (also known as scallions in eastern parts of the United States) I generally mean to include the entire onion, from the white bulb to the leafy green stalks. Mexican green onions, which are generally differentiated by their larger more developed bulbs, may be used interchangeably with the variety most commonly found in the United States.

jícama: Jícama is a large round root that, when peeled, yields a crunchy, starchy flesh similar to that of an uncooked potato or apple. Most significantly, jícama does not discolor after its skin has been removed, so it adds a lovely, bright white crunch to salads, stir fry, or atop a warm taco or burrito. In terms of both flavor and texture, water chestnuts would be the best substitute for jícama.

tomatillo: Often mistaken as green or unripe tomatoes, tomatillos are actually most closely related to the cape gooseberry. Just peel off the papery husk and slice one open to see: the interior of a tomatillo is much fleshier than a tomato with a much more dense seed pattern. Their firmness and extremely tart flavor make tomatillos the perfect candidate for a starring role in bright salsa verde. When shopping for ripe tomatillos, look for fruit that fills out or has actually split the exterior husk. Back home, be sure to wash thoroughly after removing the husk, as the fruit itself will often be covered in a sticky residue.

tomatoes: I use plum or Roma tomatoes almost exclusively when it comes to fresh tomatoes, for the simple reason that they are meatier and contain less seeds. This is especially useful when it comes to making salsas. You may substitute other types of fresh tomatoes for plum tomatoes in my recipes, but you will likely want to seed them before incorporating into a salsa or other dish.

dairy

cheddar cheese: Cheddar cheese has become almost as ubiquitous as American cheese in the United States, and whether topping tacos or lining quesadillas, it has long been associated with Southwestern cuisine. I call for sharp cheddar in recipes when I'm looking to add a cheese with a bit of a bite. As with all other cheeses that are sold commercially in both grated and block form, I strongly recommend opting for the block variety and taking the time to grate it yourself; freshly grated cheese doesn't just taste better, it melts more rapidly and more evenly.

chihuahua cheese: Chihuahua cheese is a mild, Mexican melting cheese that is most commonly used in dishes where its smooth melting properties are of benefit, such as *queso fundido*, a type of Mexican fondue, or quesadillas. Chihuahua cheese is named after the Mexican state in which it was originally produced, and is often labeled *queso menonita*. A mild cheddar or Monterey Jack cheese may be substituted for Chihuahua cheese.

cotija cheese: Cotija is a hard cow's milk Mexican cheese that has an extremely salty flavor. It is often sold in rounds or pre-crumbled or grated, similar to Parmesan cheese. When cooked, cotija will soften but will not melt, making it a wonderful topping for tacos, burritos, salads, or tostadas. Note that while cotija is usually sold in Mexico after being aged a minimum of 100 days, it is often sold much fresher in the United States. The fresher version will be slightly softer than the aged or 'añejo' variety, but it will add the same lovely salted cream tang to the dish of your choosing. Mild feta cheese makes an excellent substitute for fresh cotija, while Parmesan cheese is the perfect substitute for cotija *añejo*.

crema: *Crema* is a Mexican table cream that is used both in and on top of savory and sweet dishes. It is thicker than American heavy whipping cream and is best replaced with crème fraîche. *Crema agria* is a slightly soured version of straight *crema*, which is why it is most often consumed on top of savory dishes. Sour cream is an excellent substitute for *crema agria*, although you may wish to thin it slightly with several tablespoons of milk.

manchego cheese: Manchego is actually a Spanish cheese that has found its way into Southwestern cuisine. It is a hard sheep's milk cheese that boasts a nutty, slightly peppery flavor most closely resembling that of Parmesan or a young gruyère. Note that most Manchego sold in the United States is firm and aged, and should not be confused with Mexican '*queso tipo manchego*' or Manchego-type cheese, which is actually a cow's milk cheese similar to cheddar or colby. The best substitutes for Spanish Manchego cheese are Parmesan or Pecorino Romano cheeses.

monterey jack cheese: Monterey Jack is an American semi-hard cheese made from cow's milk and often incorporated into blends with cheddar or Colby cheeses. Varieties include pepper jack, which incorporates strips of fresh chiles, and dry jack, which is aged to a consistency similar to that of Parmesan. I most often use plain fresh Monterey Jack cheese, as I love its creamy texture and excellent melting capability.

oaxaca cheese: Oaxaca cheese, also named after the Mexican state from which it originates, is a mild cow's milk cheese. It is produced by stretching the curd and, as such, is often sold in braids and consumed in strings, similar to mozzarella. When eaten on its own, Oaxaca cheese has a chewy consistency and a creamy, slightly salty flavor. Mozzarella or Monterey Jack cheeses may be substituted for Oaxaca cheese.

queso fresco: Queso fresco is a fresh cheese typically sold in pressed rounds. The most important thing to keep in mind when working with queso fresco is that it will not melt, which is why it is usually served crumbled on top of tacos, salads, beans, or even rice. Queso fresco's firm texture and slightly acidic flavor is most closely comparable to a mild or medium feta cheese.

baking ingredients

agave nectar: Agave nectar is a thick, syrup-like sweetener extracted from the leaves of the agave plant. It is sweeter than honey and dissolves quite rapidly, which makes it an ideal additive to both baked goods and beverages. While agave nectar is sold in light, amber, dark, and raw varieties, I most often use the light as I prefer its milder flavor. Honey may be substituted for light agave nectar; maple syrup for dark or raw.

butter: I only use unsalted butter in my kitchen, especially when it comes to baking; I prefer to control the amount of salt that goes into each dish that I am preparing, an objective best achieved by simply using unsalted butter.

chocolate: Mexican chocolate is a prepared chocolate that often includes flavor additives such as almonds or almond extract, cinnamon, and vanilla. Most notably, Mexican chocolate is extremely grainy compared to American or European chocolate; it is most commonly used to prepare hot chocolate beverages or season mole sauces. Mexican chocolate is sold in packages of scored discs and has become widely available in well-stocked grocery stores throughout the United States. In a pinch, I will substitute one ounce of semisweet chocolate combined with several drops each of vanilla and almond extracts for Mexican chocolate.

cornmeal: Not to be confused with *masa harina*, cornstarch, or cornflour, cornmeal is simply the result of grinding dried corn to a fine, medium, or coarse meal. The recipes in this book generally call for the steel-ground fine yellow cornmeal that is common to local markets throughout the United States. The Hopi Blue Corn Tortillas found on page 112 are the single exception: they call for blue cornmeal, which can be found in well-stocked grocery stores and health foods markets.

dulce de leche: Dulce de leche is a traditional Mexican caramel sauce made from cow's milk, as opposed to the goat's milk that is used to produce cajeta (page 38). Dulce de leche has become quite popular in the United States in recent years, and can be purchased by the can from the Hispanic section of any well-stocked market.

eggs: Any reference that I make to eggs in this book, whether in baked goods or otherwise, refers to large eggs.

flour: The recipes in this book call exclusively for all-purpose flour. I have learned to seek out the highest quality flour possible, especially when using it to produce breads such as Pueblo Bread or even Fry Bread, as the finer flour will consistently yield a superior finished product. Although many bakers will not agree, I do not believe it is necessary to sift all-purpose flour, and instead choose to simply run it through with a whisk, often after combining with additional dry ingredients. Whisking rather than sifting is simply more practical and offers all the aeration necessary when working with all-purpose flour.

lard and shortening: Historically, most Native American and Mexican baking was done with lard or *manteca*; lard was accessible and inexpensive, and it yields a lovely dense crumb in leavened breads and an irresistible crisp crunch in fried dishes. For obvious nutritional reasons, lard has fallen out of fashion and I rarely bake with it myself. I do, however, use vegetable shortening in a number of recipes in this book, as I have found it to be a fine substitute for lard.

milks: I work with a wide variety of milks in my kitchen, from goat's milk for the cajeta found on page 38, to sweetened condensed and evaporated milks when making *tres leches* cakes such as the one found on page 211. Note that when baking I will most often use whole cow's milk or buttermilk. No buttermilk on hand? No problem. You can prepare a basic buttermilk by combining one tablespoon of distilled white vinegar with one cup of whole milk and allowing the mixture to stand on the counter in a warm kitchen for 10 to 20 minutes, or until it curdles.

nuts: Southwestern cuisine incorporates a wide variety of nuts in both their whole and ground forms. While pecans, pinyons, and walnuts are generally the only nuts indigenous to this part of the country, dishes have evolved to incorporate peanuts, pistachios, and almonds as well. Note that I will almost always toast nuts before using them in a dish, as warming is essential to highlighting their natural flavors. Please refer to individual recipes for instructions and toasting times. Pinyons are the only nut that you may struggle to locate in your local market: they are the product of pine trees that grow throughout New Mexico and can take years to develop into a crop worthy of harvesting. Pine nuts or pignolis may be substituted for pinyon nuts.

seeds: As with nuts, there are a number of seeds that are used whole in modern Southwestern cooking. The recipes in this book call for anise, chia, pumpkin, sesame, and sunflower seeds, and indicate toasting times as applicable. Be sure to pick out seeds that have already been hulled, especially when it comes to pumpkin and sunflower seeds, but not otherwise cooked or seasoned.

vanilla: I prefer to bake with Mexican vanilla when I can. Mexican vanilla beans are prized for their rich, complex flavor, and I find that even when processed into an extract, Mexican vanilla still tastes distinctly less astringent than any other variety. Unfortunately, Mexican vanilla is not as accessible in the U.S. as many of the other ingredients that I have described here, and as such, basic vanilla extract may be substituted whenever vanilla is called for in this book. I encourage you to seek out the highest quality vanilla extract that you can, as the difference in the flavor of the finished product is notable.

other pantry staples

fideos: Fideos are a type of vermicelli pasta commonly used in Mexican cuisine. You will likely find them sold dried and either 'cut' or 'coiled'. Angel hair pasta is a perfect substitute for fideos, although if a recipe calls for the 'cut' variety, as with the Fideo Burrito recipe found on page 146, you should break the angel hair into smaller pieces before cooking.

masa harina: Masa harina is one of the most important building blocks of Southwestern cuisine as it is used to prepare the corn tortillas that form the foundation of so many classic dishes. Masa harina is a corn-based flour that is produced by treating dried corn with slaked lime. Neither cornmeal nor all-purpose flour are acceptable substitutes for masa harina, since this unique process of softening the dried corn, known as nixtamalization, is requisite for yielding the finished corn flour. Thankfully, masa harina has become almost as common as flour in the United States, and can usually be found in the baking section of any well-stocked grocery store.

essential equipment

blender/food processor: Blenders and food processors are critical tools when it comes to producing salsas and sauces, and when working with fresh and dried ingredients and spices. Many people prefer to use one or the other for different tasks, but I work almost exclusively with a sturdy food processor. You may use whichever machine you have access to and are comfortable with, as long as it is fitted with a steel blade. Note that several of the recipes included in this book will yield a large volume of salsa or sauce, so depending on the capacity of your food processor or blender, you may need to work in batches.

canning jars: I generally recommend storing condiments in glass canning jars. I have found that glass containers, unlike some plastics, do not in any way alter the flavor of their contents. Glass canning jars offer the added bonus of being reusable, as well as transparent, making it easy to identify what's inside at a glance. I find glass canning jars in a variety of sizes at my local market or craft store.

comal: A comal is a smooth, flat griddle often used in Mexican cooking to warm tortillas, toast dried chiles, and even prepare meats. Comals come in a variety of sizes and shapes, although most comals used in non-commercial kitchens are either round or oval. Comals are typically made from cast iron, which is why a cast iron skillet of any shape or size is the perfect substitute for a comal.

fine mesh sieve/cheesecloth: A good quality fine mesh sieve will come in extremely handy when it comes to producing silky sauces and salsas. Look for one that is large and sturdy enough to fit over your mixing bowls as you work. In some instances, such as the Cucumber & Melon *Agua Fresca* recipe found on page 94, a cheesecloth may be used in place of a fine mesh sieve.

molcajete: Molcajetes are a sort of mortar and pestle used in many Mexican kitchens for grinding spices and preparing salsas. In the United States, molcajetes have become most commonly associated with making guacamole, probably because they are the perfect tool for achieving the best consistency, which is key when it comes to the popular avocado-based condiment. Although I have seen them made from plastic, metal, and all kinds of other materials, I personally prefer to use a more traditional molcajete made from vesicular basalt. Similar to a cast iron pan, the pitted stone surface of both the mortar (*molcajete*) and pestle (*tejolote*) retain just a bit of flavor every time it is used, so it only gets better with age. A molcajete is not a requisite tool for preparing any of the recipes in this book, but if you have the opportunity to work with one, I encourage you to do so, especially when it comes to making guacamole.

spice grinder: I strongly recommend investing in an electric spice mill. While you can grind most dried chiles, spices, seeds, and nuts by hand, you will get a much more even result when you leave the work to a machine. Spice grinders are now available at most kitchen supply stores, but if you can't find one, a coffee bean mill would work in a pinch. Just be sure to thoroughly clean your mill after each use, especially when grinding hot dried chiles.

spice jars: As with condiments, I recommend storing spices and ground dried chiles in glass containers. After taking the time to toast and grind, you'll want to store these flavor agents in containers that offer the least amount of interference with their natural properties. I find glass spice jars at my local craft or specialty spice shop.

tortilla press: Tortilla presses are key to churning out large quantities of uniform tortillas. In the United States you will most often find presses made from metal with large handles that offer excellent leverage. Simply place a ball of masa on the base, cover, push down, and uncover your perfect tortilla. I strongly recommend lining both sides of your tortilla press with parchment, plastic wrap, or wax paper to keep the masa from sticking.

building
blocks

Every school of cooking is built on its own collection of fundamental dishes, and Southwestern cuisine is no exception. The following six recipes utilize ingredients that I return to again and again, and yield condiments and foodstuffs that are requisite in any Southwestern kitchen.

The recipes included in this chapter also involve a set of techniques that are extremely important to any Southwestern cook, whether experienced or just starting out; from roasting fresh chiles to working with *masa*, these practices form the foundation of just about every dish in the Southwestern culinary canon.

If you are new to Southwestern cuisine, these building block recipes are a wonderful place to start. The salsas, breads, and meat that you will be making from scratch will enhance any dish to which they are added, while you develop a degree of comfort and familiarity that can only come from working directly with ingredients in your own kitchen. If you have experience with Southwestern cuisine, I think you will find these recipes to be invaluable new additions to your current repertoire. Either way, they are a delicious way to begin building any Southwestern spread.

roasting fresh chiles

ripe chiles roast best. Proper roasting technique actually begins in the market by selecting firm fruit with brightly colored, unmarked, slightly waxy skin. Once you have chosen your chiles, I recommend trimming off their stems since they can easily catch fire during the roasting process, especially if you're working over an open flame. You have several options when it comes to exactly how and where you roast your chiles but I usually opt to roast mine over an open flame on my gas stovetop. Having a pair of sturdy metal tongs on hand for turning and moving your chiles is key. Place a whole chile on the open flame of the stovetop and roast, turning frequently, until evenly charred. While roasting times vary depending on the size and shape of the chile, you'll want to keep a close eye on the chile as it roasts, turning and moving it with the tongs as often as necessary to produce an evenly blackened surface. Note that it is not unusual for a chile's skin to pop and crackle as it cooks. Once the chile is evenly charred, carefully remove it from the flame to either a zip-top plastic storage bag or a large bowl covered in plastic wrap. Seal the chile inside, opening only to add additional chiles for sweating. Be sure to allow your roasted chiles at least 5 minutes to sweat; their skins should be soft, soggy, shriveled, and loose. After sweating, remove to a cutting board and use a sharp knife or your fingers to scrape or peel away the blackened skin. Once you have removed as much of the skin as possible, remove the top of the chile, slice down its length vertically, lay it flat on your work surface and scrape away the exposed seed column and membranes. At this point the flesh is most commonly cut vertically into long strips known as *rajas*, which are then incorporated into a dish of your choosing, but you may use the flesh however you like.

If you prefer not to use an open flame to roast your chiles, you can roast them in your oven under the broiler. If you choose the oven-roasted route, you will need to simply halve your chiles vertically, arrange them in an even layer (cut sides facing down) on a sturdy foil-lined baking sheet and place under the broiler until charred. Then follow the instructions above for sweating and preparing.

sunday salsa

Fresh salsas are such a fundamental part of Southwestern cuisine. Whether it's their total versatility or their infinite adaptability, having a fresh salsa on hand enhances any meal at any time of the day. Then again, why wait for a meal? Digging into a hearty homemade salsa makes for the perfect snack as well. This particular version is called "Sunday Salsa" because it is consumed in such great volumes in my household that you will frequently find me spending Sunday afternoons putting up jars of the stuff for the week ahead. It's a delicious weekend ritual that you may consider adopting for your family as well.

10 cloves garlic

½ large yellow onion, coarsely chopped

4 poblano chiles, charred, peeled, stemmed, and seeded

4 jalapeño chiles, charred, peeled, stemmed, and seeded

16 plum (Roma) tomatoes, ends removed, coarsely chopped

¼ cup freshly squeezed lime juice

1 tablespoon onion powder

1 tablespoon ground cumin

salt to taste

freshly ground black pepper to taste

Place garlic and onion in the bowl of a food processor fitted with a steel blade and process to a paste. Add remaining ingredients and process until mixed and relatively smooth. You may work in batches as necessary, and consider pulse-processing this salsa so that you have more control over the consistency of the end product.

Pour the processed salsa into a large heavy-bottomed pot and bring to a boil. Reduce to a simmer and cook for 15 to 20 minutes or until the mixture has thickened slightly. Remove from heat and set aside to cool.

This salsa is best served either slightly chilled or at room temperature. You can store it, preferably in glass containers, sealed and refrigerated for up to 2 weeks. Note that this salsa tastes even better the longer it's allowed to sit.

YIELD: approximately 8 cups

working with dried chiles: First and foremost, dried chiles should always be toasted before either grinding or soaking. Toasting for just a few minutes on each side heightens and draws out the unique flavor of each chile. Before toasting, simply remove the stem from the dried pod and discard as many of the seeds as possible, leaving the remainder of the pod intact. Place the pod on a dry pan or comal that has been heated over a medium flame, and toast for just 1 to 2 minutes on each side. Note that it is not necessary to apply pressure to the body of the chile to ensure contact with the cooking surface: ambient heat is sufficient for cooking delicate dried chile flesh. The chile will deepen in color and become extremely fragrant as it cooks. Remove the toasted chile, and once cool enough to handle, either tear the flesh into pieces and grind to a powder in a spice mill or cover with water to rehydrate. When grinding, you will likely need to pick out any large pieces that remain before storing, preferably in a sealed, opaque glass container. Rehydrating chiles simply requires covering the pods with water, bringing to a boil, and cooking until they are tender and pliable, approximately 15 to 20 minutes. Be sure to reserve your soaking liquid after draining the chiles! Softened chiles are generally processed in a food processer or blender along with a portion of the reserved liquid, as in the case of the Red Chile Sauce recipe given here.

red chile sauce

10 cloves garlic

5 tablespoons + 1 teaspoon extra virgin olive oil, divided

pinch of salt for roasting, plus more for seasoning to taste

8 ounces dried New Mexico or California red chile pods, stemmed and seeded

5 tablespoons all-purpose flour

2 teaspoons ground cumin

1 teaspoon ground coriander

1 teaspoon ground oregano (preferably Mexican oregano)

1 teaspoon ground white pepper

Whether you call it enchilada sauce, red chile sauce, or *chile colorado*, this red sauce made from dried chiles is a staple in any Southwestern kitchen. Its flavor is deep and layered, showcasing the smoky, earthen heat of toasted New Mexican red chile pods, and it is incredibly versatile. I use it to punch up eggs in the morning, flavor bean quesadillas for lunch, then play the starring role in chicken enchiladas at the end of the day. You won't regret taking the time to churn out jars of this sauce to have on hand for spicing up any dish.

Preheat oven to 350°F.

Toss garlic with 1 teaspoon of olive oil and a pinch of salt, and wrap tightly in a foil packet. Roast for approximately 30 minutes, until cloves are fragrant, softened, and slightly golden. Place garlic in the bowl of a food processor fitted with a steel blade to cool.

Meanwhile, place the dried chile pods in a large heavy-bottomed stockpot over a medium flame, stirring frequently to allow even toasting. After approximately 2 to 4 minutes, once pods are darkened and fragrant, fill the pot with water and bring to a boil, stirring often to ensure chiles are submerged and cooking evenly. Boil until chiles are tender and pliable, approximately 15 to 20 minutes. Remove chiles from heat and drain, reserving 5 cups of the cooking liquid.

continued on page 28

Place the chile pods in the food processor bowl with the garlic and process to a thick paste. Once your chiles and garlic have been processed, process in the reserved cooking liquid. Once the mixture is a uniform consistency, pour through a fine-mesh sieve into a large heat-proof bowl. (Note that you may have to divide the chiles, garlic and cooking liquid in half and work in batches at this stage, if your food processor cannot accommodate all of those ingredients at once.)

Heat the remaining 5 tablespoons of olive oil in the same large heavy-bottomed stockpot over a medium flame. Add the flour to the heated oil, stirring constantly and in a circular motion until a paste forms. Stir in the cumin, coriander, oregano, and white pepper to form a smooth paste, working quickly so that the flour does not burn. Carefully stir in the strained chile mixture and bring to a boil. Continue to boil until the sauce is thick enough to coat the back of a wooden spoon, approximately 5 to 8 minutes. Remove finished sauce from heat and store in the refrigerator, preferably in sealed glass containers.

YIELD: approximately 4 cups

navajo fry bread

2 cups all-purpose flour plus
    more for dusting your hands

2 teaspoons baking powder

1 tablespoon powdered milk

½ teaspoon salt

2 cups very warm water*

1 quart vegetable oil for frying

baking as a tradition: Fry
bread is not typically flavored with
additives like conventional quick
breads—you won't find fry bread
dough being made with raisins or
carrots or seasoning of any sort.
Instead, varieties of fry bread dough
are made with alternate types of
flour, such as whole wheat flour or
blue or yellow cornmeals. Because
the dough is ultimately deep fried,
however, I have found that simple
all-purpose flour yields the best result
every single time. Be sure to mix your
dough by hand, give it a chance to
rest before shaping, and puncture
the center of each piece with your
thumb to give the finished bread a
lovely, puffy texture.

Native American breads are, in many ways, ambassadors
for traditional tribal technique and culinary tradition.
Whether it is leavened loaves baked in *hornos* or crispier
flats rolled out on hot stone, bread recipes that have been
passed down through centuries are a wonderful tool for
beginning to understand Native American cuisine, past and
present. Ironically, the bread that is most commonly known
off of the reservation is not baked: Navajo Fry Bread is
fried to perfection in fat. Served hot from the stove, fry
bread is the ideal accompaniment to, or vessel for, warm
meats, beans, and/or vegetables (see recipe for Navajo
Tacos, page 164). Or top with honey and a dusting of sugar
for an indulgent dessert or snack.

....

*Note: You want your water to be as warm as possible
without being so hot that you can't work it into the dry
ingredients with your hands.

Whisk the flour, baking powder, powdered milk, and salt
together in a large bowl. Pour in the warm water and
use your clean hands to work the water into the flour,
mixing in a circular motion. Once the water has been
completely absorbed, knead the dough for a turn or two
to form a single solid mass. It may seem that this dough
is excessively dry: 2 cups of water should be sufficient
for it to come together but if your dough absolutely isn't
solidifying, you may add additional water, 1 tablespoon
at a time. Take care not to add too much water or to
overwork your dough. Once your dough has come
together, cover it with a damp towel and set aside to rest
for 30 minutes.

When ready to fry, heat your oil in a large heavy-bottomed pot to a temperature of 350°F. Pull off a plum-size piece of dough, and using floured hands, flatten into a round shape approximately ¼ inch thick. Puncture the center of the dough with your thumb and carefully drop into the hot oil. Fry for approximately 60-90 seconds on each side until puffed, crisp, and cooked through. Finished fry bread will be crisp, puffed, and deep golden brown. Remove from oil to a paper-towel-lined surface to drain for just a few minutes and serve hot. Continue with your remaining dough.

YIELD: approximately 12 pieces of bread

working with masa: Corn tortillas are made from *masa harina*, a cornmeal flour that is specially prepared by treating dried corn with slaked lime, which softens the corn. It is important to note that this treatment process is critical to the development of *masa harina*—plain cornmeal cannot be substituted. With the simple addition of water to *masa harina*, a dough or *masa* is formed. When preparing corn tortillas, always keep any unused *masa* covered with a damp cloth so that it doesn't dry out and become unworkable. Do not substitute butter or oil for shortening when preparing flour tortillas, and never use any oil when cooking; both corn and flour tortillas should always be dry-cooked on a hot comal or griddle. Finally, always line your tortilla press or rolling pin with plastic wrap, parchment paper, or plastic bags to stop your dough from sticking.

corn tortillas

2 cup masa harina

1¾ cups warm water

special equipment: A tortilla press comes in extremely handy when shaping and pressing your tortillas, as well as plastic wrap or parchment paper for lining. A rolling pin can stand in for a press in a pinch. A comal, griddle, or large heavy-bottomed skillet will be necessary for cooking. The most important part of working with a tortilla press is the lining. I recommend taking the time to wrap both the top and the bottom of the press in order to prevent your tortillas from sticking and ripping. When preparing corn tortillas, I usually slip a plastic zip-top bag over the top of the press, and then wrap the bottom in parchment paper. When preparing flour tortillas, the sticky dough requires a bit more effort; again you'll want to line the top and bottom of your press with plastic and parchment, but then also dust a small bowl with flour and roll each ball of dough in the bowl before pressing. Coating your unpressed dough in flour makes for easier handling and does not affect the flavor or consistency of the finished product.

Preparing your own tortillas, be it flour or corn-based, may seem daunting. But don't be dissuaded: once you have the modest tools and ingredients required on hand, and a sort of production line in place, the process is not intimidating at all. And the end result, oh the end result … fresh, warm, handmade tortillas are well, well worth your effort. In addition, once you establish a familiarity with *masa*, the sky is the limit; you will have opened the door to so many wonderful *masa*-based treats, including sopes, like the ones on page 108.

Place masa harina in a large bowl and slowly pour in the warm water. Stir the mixture with a fork for several seconds and then switch to clean hands as the dough begins to come together into a ball. Knead the solid, uniform dough several times and cover with a damp cloth. Set aside to rest for 30 minutes.

After the resting period, heat your comal or griddle over a medium-high flame. Pinch off 8 to 10 plum-size balls of dough and flatten your first dough ball using a lined tortilla press or rolling pin. I find that, at this point, it is easiest to work in a production line beginning with the separated pieces of dough; you can work on pressing one tortilla as another is cooking. Cook your pressed tortilla in the heated pan for 2 minutes on one side, and then 2 to 3 minutes more on the other side. Your tortilla will be done when it begins to show brown flecks on the surface. Remove cooked tortilla to a warmer or serve immediately.

Cooked tortillas can be stored, covered, for up to several weeks in the refrigerator, although tortillas should always be allowed to return to room temperature or warmed before serving and/or stuffing.

YIELD: 8 to 10 5- to 6-inch corn tortillas

corn and flour tortillas

flour tortillas

3¾ cups all-purpose flour,
   divided, plus more for
   dusting your hands and work
   surface

2 teaspoons baking powder

¼ cup vegetable shortening

1½ cups warm water

Whisk together the dry ingredients except ¾ cup of flour in a large bowl. Using a pastry cutter or fork, cut the shortening into the dry ingredients. Slowly pour in the warm water and stir. At this point your dough will be wet, sticky, and slightly soupy. Work in remaining flour with your hands, forming a solid, uniform ball of dough.

Heat your comal or griddle over medium heat. Working on one tortilla at a time, pinch off a small ball of dough about the size of a plum and flatten it using a lined tortilla press or rolling pin. Cook your pressed tortilla in the heated pan for 2 minutes on one side, and then 2 to 3 minutes more on the other side. Your tortilla will be done when it begins to show brown flecks on the surface. Remove the cooked tortilla to a warmer or serve immediately. Continue with remaining dough.

Cooked tortillas can be stored, covered, for up to several weeks in the refrigerator, although tortillas should always be allowed to return to room temperature or warmed before serving and/or stuffing.

YIELD: 12 5- to 6-inch flour tortillas

chorizo

10 dried New Mexico red chile
   pods, stemmed and seeded

½ cup apple cider vinegar

2 tablespoons smoked paprika

1 tablespoon salt

1 tablespoon garlic powder

1 tablespoon ground white
   pepper

2 pounds ground pork

Starting from scratch when it comes to sausage just makes sense: you are the master of your own destiny when it comes to flavor, seasoning, and overall quality of the finished product. And flavor matters that much more with chorizo, as it is rarely eaten by itself; cooked chorizo is often used to punch up dishes such as eggs, beans, and warm bread, all of which benefit from the rich, savory flavor of the meat. This also explains why recipes for homemade chorizo, such as this one, generally involve hefty doses of seasoning and salt, and often incorporate the acidic bite of vinegar. Here, apple cider vinegar adds a slightly sweet taste that works well with the naturally sweet flavor of pork and the smoky heat of ground dried chiles.

Place the dried chile pods in a large heavy-bottomed stockpot over a medium flame, and stirring frequently, cook until evenly toasted, approximately 1 to 2 minutes. Once pods are darkened and fragrant, fill the pot with water and bring to a boil. Boil until chiles are tender and pliable, approximately 15 to 20 minutes, stirring often to ensure chiles are submerged and cooking evenly. Remove chiles from heat and drain, reserving ½ cup of the cooking liquid.

preparing seasoned sausage:
Cooking chorizo is the simple work of heating the sausage in a heavy-bottomed skillet over a medium flame until it is just beginning to brown. Use a wooden spoon or spatula to gently break the meat into crumbles as it cooks through, approximately 7 to 12 minutes depending on the desired degree of doneness. I prefer to cook fresh chorizo in a dry pan without any additional oil or fat.

Place chile pods in the bowl of a food processor fitted with a steel blade and process to a thick paste. Add the reserved cooking liquid, vinegar, paprika, salt, garlic powder, and pepper and process until the mixture is uniform.

Place the pork in a large bowl. Add the chile mixture and, using clean hands, gently work into the pork, taking care not to overwork the meat and to distribute the chile paste evenly throughout the ground meat.

The prepared chorizo may be stored, covered, in the refrigerator for up to one week, and is usually best after sitting for at least one day.

YIELD: approximately 2 pounds seasoned meat

cajeta

½ teaspoon baking soda

2 quarts goat's milk

2 cups dark brown sugar, firmly packed

1 teaspoon salt

1 stick canela (a stick of cinnamon may be substituted)

Freshly made cajeta is truly a revelation. Without question it is the rich, grassy flavor and fragrance of goat's milk that makes this traditional caramel sauce so incredibly unique. Cajeta is not terribly difficult to prepare, especially once you get the timing and temperature down. Which is yet another reason why for gifting, serving, slathering, and spooning directly out of the jar, I cannot recommend this luscious sweet sauce highly enough. Be sure to also try the delicious variations on page 41.

Stir the baking soda with 1 tablespoon of water in a small bowl and set aside.

Place the goat's milk, brown sugar, salt, and canela stick in a large heavy-bottomed stockpot and stir together. Bring to a boil over medium-high heat, stirring frequently.

Once you have achieved a rolling boil, remove the milk mixture from the heat and carefully add the baking soda mixture, stirring to incorporate. The milk may foam as you add the baking soda, just continue to stir gently until the foaming subsides.

Return the mixture to the heat, reduce the temperature to medium, and continue to cook, stirring occasionally, until mixture has reduced and turned a deep golden brown, approximately 1 hour and 45 minutes. It is important that the milk maintains a temperature high enough that it continues to gently boil/simmer, but not so high that it foams up and scorches. The finished cajeta will have turned a deep golden brown color and will often begin to foam once more just as it is ready to be removed from the heat. After the proper time has passed and/or the mixture has reduced and is beginning to foam again, you can test for doneness by rubbing a small bit of the

special equipment: I find that using a wooden spoon to stir the cajeta as it cooks yields the cleanest flavor in the finished product. I also strongly recommend, especially if you use a stick of canela instead of a stick of cinnamon, not skipping the final step of passing the cooked cajeta through a fine-mesh sieve. Canela is so much more delicate than whole cinnamon, and as the milk cooks your stick will likely break into small pieces that you will ultimately want to remove. A silky, smooth caramel sauce is your reward for the extra effort.

mixture against a ceramic plate. If the cajeta is finished it will be thick and viscous against the surface of the plate; simply keep cooking if it seems too thin. Once completely cooked, remove from the heat and carefully pour through a fine-mesh sieve into a large heat-proof bowl.

Transfer the strained caramel to an airtight container, preferably a large glass jar, as soon as it is cool enough to handle. Because cajeta is a milk-based product, be sure to store it in the refrigerator. I do recommend, however, allowing the sauce to return to room temperature before serving or enjoying.

YIELD: approximately 2 to 2½ cups

flavoring fresh cajeta

Cajeta (page 38) is simply too special to be restricted to making just one time of the year. I adjust the recipe to take advantage of sweet summer coconut in the first half of the year, and abundant winter citrus in the second.

to prepare coconut-infused cajeta, crack a whole coconut, reserving 1 cup of the coconut water. Grate the coconut meat. Follow instructions for the basic cajeta recipe up until the point where you have stirred in the baking soda; while the pot is still off of the heat, stir in 1 cup of the coconut meat (reserve the rest for another use). Proceed with the remainder of the recipe and just after passing the cajeta through the sieve, pour the 1 cup of coconut water through the sieve and into the cajeta. Stir to incorporate.

to prepare citrus-infused cajeta, use a sharp vegetable peeler to remove the rind from 1 whole large orange and then squeeze the juice from 2 whole oranges. Follow instructions for the basic cajeta recipe up until the point where you have stirred in the baking soda; while the pot is still off of the heat, stir in the orange rind. Proceed with the remainder of the recipe and just after passing the cajeta through the sieve, pour the orange juice through the sieve and into the cajeta. Stir to incorporate.

condiments

I make no apologies for it—I am a condiment queen. There is just something incredibly satisfying about putting up jar after jar of luscious sauces, salsas, and spreads. Of course, thoughtfully prepared condiments can really enhance any meal, and the following salsas and sauces are designed to do just that. You simply need to select the right salsa for your meal and serve it up (in many cases I have listed suggested condiment pairings within recipes).

Salsas are incredibly important to Southwestern cuisine. Meals are rarely served without them in this corner of the country. I think you will find that each of these condiments will play a specific role in your kitchen. Tart green salsa offers a bright bite, tomato-based hot sauce brings the heat, and a rich, savory cream sauce is a cool way to top off any taco or torta.

I recommend storing homemade salsas and condiments in glass canning jars. Glass containers are simply the best vessels for preserving and protecting the flavors of the fruits of your labor.

salsa verde

Tart *salsa verde* is such a wonderful compliment to just about any dish. This particular sauce gets its tang from fresh tomatillos, which are perfect for salsas since they are not overly juicy and have an extremely bright flavor. I like to round out my *salsa verde* with roasted Anaheim chiles, which add just a hint of heat and tons of smokiness to offset the pucker. Finish things off with fresh garlic and herbaceous parsley and you've got a salsa that barely even needs a chip to go with it.

4 large cloves garlic, peeled

4 Anaheim chiles, roasted, peeled, stemmed*

½ cup packed fresh parsley

8 tomatillos, husked and halved

salt to taste

*I usually opt to leave in the seeds of the chiles for this salsa, but you may remove them if you prefer less heat.

Place the whole garlic cloves in the bowl of a food processor fitted with a steel blade and process to a paste. Add the chiles and parsley and process again to a paste. Add the tomatillos and process to a smooth, even consistency. Season with salt to taste and serve. Or store in the refrigerator, covered, preferably in glass containers, for up to 3 weeks.

YIELD: approximately 3 cups

roasted garlic guacamole

6 large cloves garlic, peeled

dash of olive oil and a pinch of
   salt for roasting

4 large avocados

2 tablespoons freshly squeezed
   lime juice

½ teaspoon ground white pepper

I have seen guacamole recipes destroy relationships, divide families, and incite global conflict. Just kidding. But it does seem that while guacamole lovers can agree on their feelings about this addictive condiment, they can't seem to agree on much else. I personally feel that less is more when it comes to luscious, ripe avocados, so I add only three additional ingredients to my guacamole: freshly squeezed lime juice keeps things tart and bright, ground white pepper adds a hint of (invisible) spice, and caramelized garlic brings out the natural sweetness of fresh avocado flesh. Hopefully we can give peace a chance and agree on this particular recipe for guacamole.

....

Preheat oven to 350°F.

Wrap the whole garlic cloves sprinkled with the oil and salt tightly in a foil packet and roast for approximately 30 minutes, or until cloves are fragrant, softened, and slightly browned. Place in the bowl of a food processor fitted with a steel blade and process to a paste. Set aside.

Meanwhile, carefully slice avocados in half vertically, remove pits, and scrape flesh from skin.

Place the avocado flesh, garlic paste, lime juice, and white pepper in the bowl of a molcajete and mash, working toward an even but chunky finished product. Serve immediately.

YIELD: approximately 2 to 2½ cups

special equipment: While a molcajete is not absolutely necessary for preparing this guacamole, it is the ideal tool for achieving the best consistency. You can use a large bowl and fork or potato masher instead, but guacamole is at its best when it retains some of the original texture of the ripe avocado fruit. I definitely do not recommend mixing guacamole in a blender or food processor—you're going for a chunky finished product, not baby food.

serrano citrus hot sauce

Most hot sauces are vinegar-based, deriving their intensity from varying proportions of dried ground cayenne chile. I prefer a hot sauce that offers a little more complexity, while also bringing the heat. This tomato-based sauce is nice and spicy, but keeps things bright with doses of freshly squeezed orange and lime juice. Blended with sweet tomatoes and citrus, the fresh serrano chiles offer a moderate degree of heat without going nuclear on your palate.

....

10 serrano chiles, stemmed

2 (28 ounce) cans crushed tomatoes in puree

1 cup freshly squeezed lime juice

1 cup freshly squeezed orange juice

½ cup white vinegar

2 tablespoons garlic powder

1 tablespoon ground coriander

Submerge chiles in enough water to cover in a large heavy-bottomed pan and bring to a boil. Cook until chiles are softened, approximately 10 to 15 minutes. Remove from heat and drain.

Place chiles in the bowl of a food processor fitted with a steel blade and process to a paste. Add remaining ingredients and process until smooth and blended, approximately 30 seconds.

Working in batches as necessary, pass the processed sauce through a fine mesh sieve. You will want to use the back of a wooden spoon or rubber scraper to force the sauce through the sieve. Ultimately all you'll be left with in the sieve is a thick paste, which you can simply discard.

Store the finished sauce in bottles or jars (preferably glass, small-mouthed vessels) in your refrigerator up to one month.

YIELD: approximately 48 fluid ounces

quick pickled jícama

You've just got to love jícama—it's crunchy, it's healthy, and it's a vehicle for the flavors of your choosing, which is why I love to pickle it. Best of all, jícama does not discolor, which means you can peel it, prepare it, and season it in advance, bringing it out to top tacos, sandwiches, salads, or even soups whenever your heart desires. That really is a lot to love, no?

· ·

1 large jícama root, peeled, chopped into sticks*

1 cup white vinegar

1 cup cider vinegar

1 tablespoon freshly squeezed lime juice

2 tablespoons coriander seeds

1 tablespoon fennel seeds

1 tablespoon black peppercorns

1 tablespoon granulated white sugar

½ teaspoon salt

*Note: Your average vegetable peeler will likely not be durable enough to peel jícama, as you need to remove both the yellow exterior skin and the fibrous layer underneath. Instead, use a sharp knife to carefully peel the root, slice it in half, and then chop into sticks sized to fit your pickling jars.

Fill each of your three sterilized jars with the prepared jícama sticks and set aside.

Place the remaining ingredients and 1 cup of water in a heavy-bottomed stockpot and bring to a boil. Boil until sugar and salt have dissolved, approximately 2 minutes. Remove from heat and carefully ladle hot pickling solution over the jícama, leaving approximately 1 inch of headspace in each jar and distributing the seeds as evenly as possible among the three containers.

Set aside to cool before sealing and storing in the refrigerator. Note that the flavor of this pickled jícama deepens the longer it is allowed to sit. Note also that these are not technical canning instructions, which is why these pickles should be stored in the refrigerator where they will keep for up to one month. This works out well, though, as I have found that jícama is best enjoyed chilled.

YIELD: approximately 3 pints

special equipment: While I advocate storing just about every type of homemade condiment in glass jars, I think this is especially important when it comes to pickled preparations. I recommend having three sterilized wide-mouth pint-size glass canning jars on hand for this particular recipe.

whipped agave ancho butter

1 cup (2 sticks) unsalted butter, softened*

2 tablespoons light agave nectar

1 tablespoon ground dried ancho chile

2 teaspoons garlic powder

1 teaspoon vanilla extract

½ teaspoon ground white pepper

*Butter whips best when it is at room temperature; take the extra time to be sure your butter is truly completely softened before preparing this recipe.

I love keeping a spicy, flavorful compound butter on hand, and this version is my personal favorite. The ingredients might seem a little odd (vanilla with white pepper?) but trust me, they work. The finished butter is light and fluffy with a lovely sweet and savory kick. Smear it on dinner rolls, melt it over savory griddle cakes, or use it to elevate your next slice of toast. Either way, you'll love how easy this flavored butter is to prepare, and you'll really love finding it in your fridge the next time you're looking for something special to finish your meal.

Place all of the ingredients in the bowl of a stand mixer fitted with a whisk attachment. Begin mixing on low speed just to incorporate ingredients. Once ingredients are loosely mixed, increase mixer speed to high and whip butter until smooth, homogeneous, and doubled in volume, approximately 2 to 3 minutes. Store in the refrigerator in a sealed, preferably glass, container.

YIELD: approximately 2 to 2½ cups

roasted crema

In our house this sauce is simply known as "that crazy-good cream salsa with lots of roasted stuff in it." Indelicate, for sure, but actually an excellent description of this sumptuous condiment. Note that your finished *crema* will be thinner than sour cream, but so much more versatile. You can use it as a dip, a sandwich spread, or even a salad dressing. Wherever you apply it, prepare for creamy, rich roasted flavor a-go-go.

5 large plum (Roma) tomatoes, ends removed, sliced approximately ½ inch thick horizontally

extra virgin olive oil for roasting

salt for roasting, and for seasoning to taste

1 large shallot, ends removed, bulbs sliced approximately ½ inch thick horizontally

4 large cloves garlic

½ cup chopped chives

2 cups crema

....

Preheat the oven 350°F.

Place tomato slices in an even layer on a parchment-lined baking sheet and drizzle lightly with olive oil. Roast for approximately 75 minutes or until tomato pieces are shrunken, dried, and just starting to char at the edges. Remove from oven and place in the bowl of a food processor fitted with a steel blade.

Meanwhile, place shallot slices and whole garlic cloves in a foil packet and toss with a light drizzle of olive oil and a pinch of salt. Wrap tightly and roast for approximately 30 minutes, until fragrant, softened, and slightly browned. Remove from oven and place in the food processor bowl with the tomatoes.

Add the chives and *crema* to the food processor bowl and process all ingredients to a smooth consistency. Season with salt to taste and serve, or store in the refrigerator, preferably in a glass container.

YIELD: approximately 3 to 4 cups

spiced corn relish

6 cups whole fresh corn kernels (uncooked)

1 cup finely diced green onions, ends removed

1 cup stemmed, seeded, finely diced red bell pepper

3 serrano chiles, stemmed, minced

½ cup minced cilantro

1 cup white vinegar

1 cup granulated white sugar

¾ cup freshly squeezed lemon juice

1½ teaspoons salt

Instead of thinking "What could I top with this relish?" ask yourself "What can't I top with this relish?" Because as flavorful as this sweet, savory, crunchy condiment is, you may just end up skipping the main course underneath and eating it straight out of the jar. And since it's just as colorful and festive as it is versatile, this relish also makes a lovely homemade gift done up in labeled glass canisters. That is, if you're willing to part with it.

Place all of the ingredients plus 2 cups of water in a heavy-bottomed stockpot and bring to a boil. Reduce to a simmer and cook until sugar and salt have dissolved and corn is tender, approximately 10 to 15 minutes.

Remove from heat and carefully ladle into prepared jars, leaving approximately 1 inch of headspace in each jar. Set aside to cool before sealing and storing in the refrigerator. Serve chilled or at room temperature.

The flavor of this relish deepens the longer it is allowed to sit. Note also that these are not technical canning instructions, which is why this relish should be stored in the refrigerator.

YIELD: approximately 7 to 8 cups

special equipment: While I advocate storing just about every type of homemade condiment in glass jars, this is especially important when it comes to pickled preparations. I recommend having two sterilized quart-size glass canning jars on hand for this particular recipe.

breakfast

Breakfast is admittedly my favorite meal of the day, which is why each of the recipes in this chapter is a true labor of love. And because everyone deserves to have choices first thing in the morning, I have included a variety of both sweet and savory dishes.

I also like to think a bit outside of the box when it comes to breakfast: starting the morning off with a meal that gets your blood pumping is the best way to wake up, don't you think? Which is why doughnuts made from fresh avocados, sweet breakfast cookies, and cheesy apple and sausage-topped pizza are often on the breakfast table in my house. The southwest landscape offers so many fresh ingredients—from juicy citrus fruits to hearty pinto beans and even earthy mushrooms—that can form a delicious foundation for that first meal of the day.

You'll likely find that many of these recipes produce quite of bit of food, which means you can either serve a crowd or have leftovers waiting for you in the refrigerator tomorrow. Delicious breakfast served up in minutes? Surely that's worth getting out of bed for!

mushroom & leek migas

4 5-inch corn tortillas

1¼ cups vegetable oil, divided

10 large eggs

¼ cup heavy cream

salt to taste

freshly ground black pepper to taste

8 ounces brown baby bella (crimini) mushrooms, brushed clean, sliced (approximately 2½ cups)

1 leek, ends removed, chopped

2 tablespoons minced fresh garlic

1 cup shredded Manchego cheese

Migas, which translates to 'crumbs' in English, literally brings everything to the table: fluffy eggs, crispy fried tortilla strips, and creamy melted cheese. This version gets an extra dose of flavor from meaty mushrooms, fresh garlic, and delicate leeks, all sautéed together to perfection. Expressly designed to serve a crowd out of one single pot, it doesn't get any easier, or more delicious, than *migas* in the morning.

To prepare the corn strips, cut the tortillas in half and then slice them into thin strips (½-inch to ¾-inch wide). Heat 1 cup of vegetable oil in a large, heavy-bottomed sauté pan over medium-high heat. Working in batches, fry the tortilla strips for 1 to 2 minutes, flipping the pieces as they fry and removing the crispy, browned strips to a paper towel-lined baking sheet to drain and cool.

Whisk the eggs and heavy cream together in a large bowl and season liberally with salt and pepper. Set aside.

Rinse out the pan used for the tortilla strips and warm the remaining ¼ cup oil over medium heat. Sauté the mushroom slices for approximately 3 minutes or until tender and fragrant. Add the leek and sauté for an additional 2 minutes. Add the garlic and sauté for 1 more minute. Pour in the egg mixture and cook, stirring constantly in a circular motion until eggs begin to solidify. Just as eggs are beginning to solidify, stir in the fried tortilla strips. Continue cooking, stirring frequently, until eggs are light, fluffy, and cooked through.

Remove from heat, top with the cheese, and serve immediately.

YIELD: approximately 4 to 6 servings

keeping avocados green: There are a lot of theories about the best way to keep fresh avocado flesh from browning after peeling. I've heard everything from keeping the pit mixed in with the flesh to coating pieces lightly with mayonnaise. After peeling more than a few avocados I have found that the best way to retain that luscious bright green color is to immediately toss the peeled flesh with freshly squeezed lime juice (approximately 1 teaspoon per avocado); the acidic citrus juice will slow the oxidation process, which is what leads to discoloration. Plus fresh, tart lime is a wonderful flavor pairing with avocado, whether you're keeping things sweet or savory.

sweet glazed avocado doughnuts

Avocados are an extremely important part of Southwestern cuisine. And it's no wonder, considering our neighbor to the south is the world's largest supplier. While most people consider avocados to be the perfect base for or compliment to a savory dish, I think their rich, creamy flavor works wonderfully in sweet preparations as well. Take these fluffy glazed doughnuts for example … I dare you to make a batch and eat just one. Double dog dare you.

....

For the doughnuts:

cooking spray

3 large avocados (1½ cups mashed)

1 tablespoon freshly squeezed lime juice

1 cup unsalted butter, softened

1 cup granulated white sugar

2 large egg yolks

½ cup whole milk

½ cup vegetable oil

4 cups all-purpose flour

1 tablespoon baking powder

½ teaspoon salt

For the coconut frosting:

3 cups confectioners' sugar

½ cup coconut milk

½ cup whole milk

special equipment: You will need one or two 6-cavity doughnut pans to make this recipe.

Preheat the oven to 350°F.

Grease one or two 6-cavity doughnut pan(s) with cooking spray and set aside.

Remove skins and pits from avocados and slice into large chunks. Place chunks in a small bowl and mash with a fork. Toss with lime juice and set aside.

In a large bowl, cream butter and sugar. Add the egg yolks, milk, and oil, and mix until fully incorporated. Mix in the avocado mash (there will be some small chunks of avocado visible in the batter).

In another bowl, whisk together flour, baking powder, and salt. Gradually add dry ingredients to wet ingredients, beating until just combined; your finished batter will be thick and quite stiff.

Fill a piping bag with the batter and pipe batter into doughnut cavities in pan, filling just to the top of each cavity. (Don't have a piping bag on hand? Simply scoop the batter into a gallon-sized zip-top bag and snip off one of the bottom corners: piping bag in a pinch!)

continued on page 65

Bake doughnuts for 12 minutes or until they are just starting to turn a very light golden brown color at the edges. Remove from oven and immediately invert the pan to release. Allow doughnuts to cool before frosting. Continue baking doughnuts until all the batter is used.

Meanwhile, whisk together confectioners' sugar, coconut milk, and whole milk until a smooth, even glaze forms.

To frost, simply dip a teaspoon into the frosting and generously coat the tops of each doughnut with the frosting.

YIELD: approximately 20 doughnuts

citrus smoothie breakfast cookies

For the cookies:

3 cups all-purpose flour, plus more for dusting

2 teaspoons baking powder

1 teaspoon salt

12 tablespoons unsalted butter, softened

1 cup firmly packed light brown sugar

2 teaspoons vanilla extract

4 large eggs

For the citrus curd:

10 large egg yolks

2 cups white sugar, granulated

½ cup freshly squeezed orange juice

½ cup freshly squeezed lemon juice

½ cup freshly squeezed lime juice

½ teaspoon salt

½ cup unsalted butter, cold, cubed

Cookies for breakfast? Indeed! In fact, you must! Especially when cookies for breakfast involves fresh, tart citrus curd sandwiched between crisp little wafers. These lovely cookies will satisfy both your sweet tooth and your busy schedule, since they are lusciously sugared as well as perfectly portable. Pack them for a breakfast on the go or save them for a sweet snack later in the day—if you can wait that long!

To prepare the cookie dough, whisk the flour, baking powder, and salt together in a large bowl and set aside. Cream the butter and brown sugar together until light and fluffy. Beat in the vanilla and add the eggs one at a time. Slowly beat in dry ingredients, mixing just until you have a stiff, uniform dough. Shape the dough into a large disk and refrigerate for 1 hour or until completely chilled through.

To prepare the curd, place the egg yolks and sugar in a large heat-proof bowl and whisk together until smooth. Whisk in the citrus juices. Fill a large saucepan halfway with water and bring to a simmer over medium-high heat. Set the bowl containing the citrus mixture over the simmering water (your saucepan should be large enough to hold your bowl directly over the simmering water without the bottom of the bowl coming into contact with the water). Whisk continuously until the mixture has thickened enough to coat the back of a wooden spoon, approximately 10 minutes. Remove from heat and immediately whisk in the salt and the butter, one piece at a time. Cover finished curd by laying plastic wrap directly on top of the surface of the curd and store in the refrigerator until ready to assemble your cookies.

Once the dough is chilled through, preheat the oven to 350°F. Using a well-floured rolling pin, roll dough out on a floured work surface to a thickness of ¼ inch. Cut out cookies using a 2½-inch round cutter and place on parchment-lined baking sheets at least 2 inches apart. Bake cookies for 15 to 16 minutes or until crisp and just beginning to brown at the edges. Remove cookies to a rack or a sheet of parchment paper and set aside to cool. Repeat until all the dough has been used.

To assemble your cookie sandwiches, spread curd generously over half of the cookies and then top each with another cookie. (This recipe yields approximately 3½ cups of curd. After assembling the cookies, you will likely have leftover curd that you can store, covered, in the refrigerator for later use.) Serve cookies immediately or store, covered, for up to one week.

YIELD: approximately 22 cookies

pinto bean breakfast patty melts

2 tablespoons extra virgin olive oil, divided, plus more for frying

¾ cup diced yellow onion

1 cup grated zucchini

2 jalapeños, stemmed and minced

2 tablespoons minced fresh garlic

3½ cups cooked pinto beans (either canned or freshly prepared)

¾ cup plain dry breadcrumbs

2 large eggs, beaten

2 tablespoons ground cumin

2 tablespoons freshly ground black pepper

1 teaspoon ground coriander

1 teaspoon salt

7 slices Monterey Jack cheese

7 English muffins, sliced, toasted

Ready for a hearty breakfast? Today's your lucky day! This twist on a classic patty melt is the perfect way to start a busy morning. Flavored mashed pinto beans offer an excellent meatless alternative to the traditional hamburger. And when formed into patties, lightly fried to a crisp, then topped with creamy Monterey Jack cheese, there's just nothing like it. Finish everything off on a toasted English muffin and you've got enough fuel in the tank to keep you happy and charged with energy for hours.

Heat 1 tablespoon of the oil in a large heavy-bottomed skillet over medium heat. Add the onion and sauté until golden, translucent, and fragrant, approximately 5 minutes. Add the zucchini, jalapeños, and garlic and sauté for just 2 more minutes. Remove pan from heat.

Meanwhile, place the beans in a large, heat-proof bowl and mash with a fork or potato masher. (I prefer to use a fork here for a chunky, uneven consistency.) Stir in the breadcrumbs, eggs, cumin, black pepper, coriander, and salt. Fold in the cooked onion mixture. Using a half cup measure, portion off and form seven 'burgers'. Refrigerate if not using right away.*

Once ready to cook and assemble your melts, heat 1 tablespoon of oil in a large heavy-bottomed, lidded skillet over medium heat. Add the patties and cook for 3 to 4 minutes on each side, applying pressure to the top of the patties to flatten once you have a cooked side facing up. Note that you may need to work in batches so as not to overcrowd your pan, so you may need to refresh your oil between batches.

*Note: These patties can be made in advance. I will often make the patty mixture on a Sunday and then fry them up for breakfasts throughout the week. If you form the patties in advance, you simply need to separate them with parchment paper so that they don't stick to each other. Store in the refrigerator until ready to cook and serve.

Once patties are crisp on the outside and cooked through, top each with a slice of cheese, replace the lid on the pan and steam just 30 to 60 seconds to melt the cheese. Remove each patty melt to a toasted English muffin bun and serve immediately.

YIELD: 7 patty melt sandwiches

sonoran honey streusel coffee cake

Honey harvested from the Sonoran Desert has such a special flavor, replete with the delicate taste and fragrance of the cactus blooms and mesquite trees that pepper the desert floor. If you don't have access to fresh Sonoran honey take the opportunity to track down honey that has been locally produced in your neighborhood. Local honey is a sweet vehicle for all of the flavors that are unique to your regional climate, which is what makes it so fun to sample and incorporate into baked goods like this sinfully rich coffee cake.

For the cake:

½ cup unsalted butter, softened

1 cup granulated white sugar

2 large eggs

1 teaspoon vanilla extract

2 cups all-purpose flour

1 teaspoon baking powder

1 teaspoon ground canela
(ground cinnamon may be substituted)

½ teaspoon salt

⅔ cup Sonoran honey (or a locally made honey from your area)

⅔ cup buttermilk

For the topping:

6 tablespoons unsalted butter, chilled and cubed

1 cup firmly packed light brown sugar

¼ cup all-purpose flour

Preheat oven to 350°F.

Line a 9-inch square baking pan with parchment paper and set aside.

To prepare the cake, cream the butter and sugar together until light and fluffy, approximately 5 minutes. Add the eggs and vanilla extract, and continue to mix just until incorporated.

Whisk the flour, baking powder, canela, and salt together in a medium bowl. Add the dry ingredients to the butter mixture in parts, alternating with the honey and then the buttermilk, mixing just until a uniform batter has formed. Pour batter into prepared pan.

To prepare the topping, in a small bowl, use your fingers to combine the butter, brown sugar, and flour into a uniform crumbled mixture. Sprinkle the topping evenly over the cake batter.

Bake for 40 to 45 minutes or until a cake tester inserted into the center of the cake comes out clean. The finished cake will be deep golden brown across the top, with the edges pulling away slightly from the sides of the pan and the topping will be melted and light golden brown. Remove baked cake from oven and set aside to cool slightly before removing from pan and serving.

YIELD: 1 9-inch square coffee cake

coconut crunch muffins

Let's face it, when muffins are good, they are so, so good. But when they are bad, they are … tragically uninspired. Luckily, these muffins are of the former variety, thanks to two different forms of coconut and the addition of a layer of lovely toasted crunch. The nutty crunch is held together with melted white chocolate, which doesn't hurt in the flavor department either. So, so good …

For the crunch:

½ cup chopped pecans

¾ cup dried shredded unsweetened coconut

¾ cup chopped vanilla wafer cookies

½ cup chopped white chocolate, melted

For the muffins:

3 cups all-purpose flour

1 teaspoon baking soda

2 teaspoons baking powder

½ teaspoon salt

1½ cups granulated white sugar

1 cup vegetable oil

2 large eggs

1 teaspoon vanilla extract

1 cup coconut milk

1 cup plain Greek yogurt

To prepare the crunch, preheat the oven to 250°F. Toss the pecans, coconut, and cookie pieces in a small bowl to blend. Add the white chocolate and continue to toss (using a rubber scraper or fork as the chocolate may still be hot) until small clusters form. Spread the clusters on a parchment-lined baking sheet and bake for 15 minutes. Finished crunch will be slightly browned and fragrant. Set aside to cool.

To prepare the muffins, whisk the flour, baking soda, baking powder, and salt together in a medium-size bowl and set aside. Cream the sugar and vegetable oil together in another larger bowl. Add the eggs one at a time, then the vanilla, beating until incorporated. Add the dry ingredients to the sugar mixture, alternating with the coconut milk, scraping down the sides of the bowl as necessary and beating until just incorporated. Beat in the yogurt.

Preheat oven to 350°F.

Line two muffin tins with paper liners and spoon or scoop the batter into the prepared muffin tin, filling each cavity just one-third of the way full (you will have some batter left). Using your hands, gently break up the crunch clusters and spoon 1 heaping teaspoon over the top of the batter in each cavity. Top the crunch with approximately 1 tablespoon more of batter. The crunch does not need to be completely covered but each liner should be filled to the top. Bake for 24 to 26 minutes, finished muffins will be slightly browned at the edges and golden across the top. Allow muffins to cool slightly before removing from pan.

YIELD: approximately 24 muffins

caramel-soaked mexican chocolate pancakes

2 disks (approximately 6.3 ounces) Mexican chocolate

1¼ cups all-purpose flour

1 tablespoon granulated white sugar

1 teaspoon baking powder

½ teaspoon baking soda

½ teaspoon salt

1¼ cups buttermilk

1 large egg

2 tablespoons vegetable oil + more for frying

1 teaspoon vanilla extract

½ teaspoon almond extract

cajeta (see page 38)

melting chocolate: Because Mexican chocolate is so naturally grainy, it is not only acceptable but preferred to skip the bain-marie and temper in the microwave. Simply chop each disk into wedges and place in a microwave-safe bowl. Cook in 30 second bursts, stirring in between, until the chocolate is the consistency of a thick paste. The finished product can be incorporated into virtually any dish of your choosing, from mole sauce to baked bread and cakes.

Mexican chocolate is a wonderful tool for elevating everyday pancakes to a whole new level. The sweet, spicy flavor of the chocolate pairs wonderfully with the fluffy texture of freshly griddled cakes. This recipe calls for vanilla and almond extracts, which really bring out the unique taste of Mexican chocolate. I serve these pancakes drenched in cajeta, hence the name.

To prepare the chocolate, chop each disk into large wedges and place in a microwave-safe bowl. Cook in two 30-second bursts, stirring after each, then finish with an additional 15 to 30 seconds. Set aside to cool slightly.

To prepare the pancake batter, whisk together the flour, sugar, baking powder, baking soda, and salt in a large bowl. In another bowl, whisk together the buttermilk, egg, 2 tablespoons of oil, vanilla extract, and almond extract. Whisk the wet ingredients into the dry ingredients, mixing just until you have a smooth, uniform batter. Slowly stir in the melted chocolate, mixing until completely distributed throughout the batter.

Heat 1 teaspoon oil in a heavy-bottomed skillet over medium heat (assuming you will be frying these pancakes in batches, I recommend adding approximately 1 teaspoon of oil to your pan at a time). Then, using a ¼-cup measure (a self-ejecting scoop comes in really handy here and ensures that all of your pancakes are evenly sized), portion out two or three pancakes. Fry pancakes for approximately 2 minutes on the first side, until air holes appear at the edges of each pancake and they are puffed and matte colored. Flip and cook 1 to 2 minutes more, until pancakes are cooked through. Stack on a plate, top with a generous drizzle of cajeta, and serve immediately. Add more oil to pan and continue to cook pancakes until all the batter is used.

YIELD: approximately 10 large pancakes

apple, cheddar & chorizo breakfast pizza

For the dough:*

1 packet (¼ ounce) dry active yeast

1 teaspoon granulated white sugar

1 teaspoon salt

1¼ cups warm water, divided

3 cups all-purpose flour plus more for dusting your work surface

For the topping:

3 Honeycrisp apples, peeled, cored, and coarsely chopped

1 cup apple juice or apple cider

3 tablespoons firmly packed dark brown sugar

2 teaspoons freshly squeezed lemon juice

1 teaspoon ground canela (ground cinnamon may be substituted)

½ teaspoon ground nutmeg

1½ teaspoons fennel seeds

1½ cups cooked chorizo (see page 36)

2 cups grated sharp orange cheddar cheese

If having pizza for breakfast is wrong, I don't want to be right. Especially when it's topped with this playful savory/sweet blend of cooked apples and chorizo. Of course, pizza isn't pizza unless it's generously dusted with cheese, and sharp yellow cheddar fills the bill nicely here. Note that this particular pizza dough does not require any kneading, so don't worry about having to break a sweat before the sun comes up.

....

*Note: This dough recipe yields enough to produce 3 large pizza crusts, but this topping recipe will only produce enough to top one pizza. You can choose to triple the topping recipe and make three pizzas at once, or simply seal the two remaining balls of dough in plastic zip-top bags and freeze for up to one month.

To prepare the dough, dissolve yeast, sugar, and salt in a small bowl with ¼ cup of the warm water. Set aside to bloom for about 5 to 10 minutes. Once yeast has bloomed, transfer mixture to a large bowl. Add the remaining 1 cup warm water. Add in the flour, 1 cup at a time, mixing well after each addition, until you have a cohesive mass of dough. Shape the dough into a large ball, cover with a damp cloth and set aside in a warm area of your kitchen to rise and double in volume, approximately 60 to 90 minutes (keep in mind that this time can vary depending on the conditions in your kitchen).

Once dough has risen, transfer to a well-floured work surface and divide into 3 portions. Cover and set aside to rest for 1 hour. After an hour, place 2 of the balls in plastic zip-top bags and freeze for later use. Place the remaining ball of dough on a parchment-lined baking sheet and gently flatten using clean hands. Working

out from the center of the dough, stretch it into a large rectangle shape by pressing firmly with your fingers until it is approximately ½ inch thick. Set aside to rest and preheat the oven to 450°F.

Meanwhile, to prepare the topping, put the apples, apple juice, brown sugar, lemon juice, canela, and nutmeg in a large heavy-bottomed skillet over medium heat. Cook, stirring often, until apples are softened and a chunky sauce forms, approximately 10 to 12 minutes. Remove pan from heat and set aside to cool slightly. Once cool, transfer to the bowl of a food processor fitted with a steel blade. Pulse-process to a smooth/chunky consistency (you can control exactly how smooth your applesauce is by simply pulse-processing and watching closely). Stir in the fennel seeds.

Spread finished applesauce generously over crust, top with chorizo crumbles, and finish with cheddar cheese. Bake for approximately 15 minutes or until cheese is melted and bubbling and crust is crisp and golden brown.

YIELD: one 10-inch or 12-inch pizza

breakfast tostadas with cumin-roasted fingerling potatoes

For the potatoes:

1½ pounds fingerling potatoes, halved vertically*

1 tablespoon extra virgin olive oil

1½ teaspoons ground cumin

½ teaspoon ground ancho chile

½ teaspoon ground coriander

salt and black pepper to taste

For the tostadas:

vegetable oil for frying the tortillas and eggs

6 4-inch corn tortillas (pre-fried, store-bought tostada shells can also be used here)

6 large eggs

1 cup shredded Manchego cheese

1 cup quartered cherry tomatoes

*Because fingerling potatoes can vary quite a bit in size and you want them to roast evenly, I always pick out any potatoes that are particularly undersized or oversized. You can save them for later use in a mashed preparation.

Tostadas, crispy fried tortillas stacked high with the toppings of your choice, are such a wonderful way to do breakfast. And because they are infinitely customizable, tostada shells with all the fixings can also serve as the perfect main event in an easy breakfast buffet. This particular take on the tostada is my absolute favorite: a fried egg, flavorful roasted fingerling potatoes, sharp Manchego cheese, and fresh cherry tomatoes. If that's not a fantastic way to start your day, I don't know what is.

....

Note: When I am preparing these tostadas for a crowd I will roast the potatoes in advance, heat the oven just to warm, assemble the tostadas on a sheet tray, and keep them hot in the oven while chopping the tomatoes and any other fresh ingredients that I might decide to add at the last minute.

To prepare the potatoes, preheat the oven to 425°F. Toss the halved potatoes, olive oil, cumin, ancho, and coriander together in a large zip-top bag until all the potato pieces are well-coated. Season with salt and black pepper to taste. Transfer the potato pieces, cut-side up, to a large nonstick or parchment-lined baking sheet. Roast the potatoes until browned and crusted on top and fork-tender inside, approximately 40 to 50 minutes. Remove from oven and set aside to cool slightly.

To prepare the tostada shells, heat approximately ½ inch of vegetable oil in a heavy-bottomed skillet over high heat. Carefully add the tortillas to the hot oil, working in batches so as not to crowd your pan. Fry each tortilla for just 30 to 60 seconds per side, or until golden brown and crisp. Remove cooked tostada shells to paper towels to drain thoroughly.

continued on next page

To prepare the eggs, heat 1 tablespoon of oil over medium heat in another large heavy-bottomed skillet. Crack your eggs into your heated skillet, again taking care not to crowd your pan and working in batches as necessary. Cook until whites are set, with the edges just beginning to curl. I like my eggs for these tostadas sunny side up, but if you prefer over easy, simply flip approximately halfway through cooking, once whites are set.

To assemble your tostadas, simply top each shell with a cooked egg, a handful of roasted potatoes, and a generous sprinkling of shredded cheese. Finish with chopped tomato pieces and serve.

YIELD: 6 tostadas

pinyon butter oatmeal

½ cup pinyon nuts

1 teaspoon honey

1 teaspoon vanilla extract

2½ cups whole milk

½ cup heavy cream

¼ cup agave nectar

1 tablespoon granulated white
   sugar

1 teaspoon ground canela
   (cinnamon may be
   substituted)

¼ teaspoon ground cloves

1½ cups old-fashioned oats

pinyon or piñon nuts are the
edible seed of a variety of species
of pinyon pine trees that flourish
throughout New Mexico, Nevada,
and Colorado. While related to
other types of pine nuts and
pignolis, American pinyon nuts are
differentiated by their larger size.
Unfortunately, pinyon nuts are often
difficult to source, due in large part
to a dwindling supply of pinyon pine
trees, which are not farmed, but
instead left to grow wild. European or
Asian pine nuts may be substituted
for pinyon nuts.

While undeniably a hearty and healthful way to start
your day, oatmeal could use a little help in the flavor
department. Enter pinyon nut butter, made from scratch in
a matter of minutes in your food processor. The toasted,
pulverized nuts boast a luscious buttery flavor and add
just the right amount of rich warmth to your morning oats.
Finish things off with a bit of sweet agave nectar and
the deep spice of both canela and cloves, and breakfast
becomes anything but a chore.

To prepare the pinyon butter, spread the nuts in an even
layer in a small, dry skillet and toast over a medium
flame, tossing often, until nuts are darkened and fragrant,
approximately 3 to 5 minutes. Place toasted nuts in the
bowl of a food processor fitted with a steel blade and
process for 10 seconds. Process 10 seconds more to a
moist, coarse meal, scraping down the sides of the bowl.
Add honey and vanilla and process to the consistency of
butter. Set aside.

To prepare the oats, place the milk, cream, agave nectar,
sugar, canela, and cloves into a large, heavy-bottomed
pot and bring to a boil. Reduce to low and stir in the
oats and nut butter. Continue to cook over low heat until
the mixture has thickened and moisture is absorbed,
approximately 8 to 10 minutes. Remove from heat and
serve immediately.

YIELD: approximately 4 servings

drinks

Beverages are often so neglected at meals and parties and just don't deserve 'afterthought' status. I have often found that adding a festive drink or two to my offerings at a party is the detail that guests later remember best. And how grateful are you when you return home after a long day and find a pitcher of something refreshing waiting for you in your refrigerator? (HINT: Very)

Drinks really set the tone for an event or occasion, which is why I try never to forget about them. In fact, when you're really in party planning mode, many of these colorful drinks can even form the foundation for a fun decorating color scheme. Won't your guests be excited when you join them with a tray of glasses filled to the brim with something sparkly and bright? (HINT: Yes)

Also, with the possible exception of Michelada, each of the alcoholic drinks in this chapter can be made without alcohol and served to thirsty tablemates of all ages.

michelada

Michelada is a bracing Mexican beer-based cocktail that brings new meaning to the term 'hair of the dog.' This version is particularly spicy, deriving its heat from both a hefty dose of hot sauce and a fresh jalapeño garnish. Batch it up to serve by the pitcher-full and then pour into salt-rimmed glasses. This drink is guaranteed to get the party started—and keep it going and going and going.

ice

12 ounces (1½ cups) light amber beer, preferably Mexican

4 ounces (½ cup) tomato juice

2 teaspoons Worcestershire sauce

1 teaspoon hot sauce (a vinegar-based hot sauce works best here)

juice of 1 fresh lime

½ jalapeño, stemmed, sliced horizontally into thin rounds*

coarsely ground salt

freshly ground black pepper, for garnish

*Your call on whether to remove the seeds from the jalapeño or not, depending on your heat tolerance, or simply omit the jalapeño altogether if you wish to further reduce the heat.

Fill a large shaker or pitcher with ice and stir in the beer, tomato juice, Worcestershire sauce, hot sauce, and lime juice. Stir in the jalapeño slices and set aside.

Meanwhile, spread the salt out onto a saucer and moisten the rim of two highball (or equivalently sized) glasses (I like to cut the lime that I just juiced into wedges and rub the still-moist citrus flesh around the tops of the glasses). Invert each glass and firmly press it into the salt until each rim is thoroughly coated. Pour the mixed drink into the prepared glasses, taking care not to disturb the salt rim, garnish each with a pinch of freshly ground black pepper and serve.

YIELD: 2 drinks

paloma

coarse salt for garnish (optional)

lime wedge for garnish (optional)

ice

2 ounces (¼ cup) mezcal

4 ounces (½ cup) freshly squeezed grapefruit juice

2 ounces (¼ cup) freshly squeezed lime juice

1 teaspoon light agave nectar

4 ounces (½ cup) club soda (seltzer water may be substituted)

mezcal: Mezcal, tequila's lesser known cousin, is often confused with tequila north of the border; but tequila is actually a form of mezcal. Both are distilled from the agave plant, mezcal from a variety of agave plants including the maguey, and tequila exclusively from the blue agave plant. There are also significant differences in the production methods of tequila versus mezcal, not the least of which being that tequila production is limited to certain regions of Mexico. You may have seen bottles of mezcal labeled as con gusano, or containing a worm. This worm is actually the larva of a moth that lives on the agave plant and inclusion in the finished liquor is nothing more than a marketing ploy. While it is always a good idea to seek out and serve high quality liquors, this is especially true of mezcal.

The Paloma is a popular Mexican cocktail that puts the 'fresh' in refreshing: a combination of citrus juices and effervescent soda water make it just the ticket for cooling off after a hard, hot day. This version of the traditionally tequila-based drink calls for mezcal instead; I find that the slightly sweeter flavor of good quality mezcal works wonderfully with fresh grapefruit and lime juices. Palomas can easily be made into a delightful virgin beverage by simply omitting the alcohol.

. . . .

Place the salt in a saucer. Moisten the rim of a highball glass with a lime wedge and firmly press it into the salt, continuing until the rim is thoroughly coated. Invert the glass and carefully fill with ice. Pour the mezcal, grapefruit juice, lime juice, and agave nectar over the ice and stir. Top off with the soda and then a lime wedge and serve.

YIELD: 1 drink

sangrita

Poor sangrita, so misunderstood … so often confused with the Spanish wine and fruit-based beverage known as sangria. Luckily for us, the tradition of true sangrita is alive and well. Sangrita is a non-alcoholic beverage originating in Mexico as an accompaniment to a straight shot of tequila blanco. Old school sangrita would typically contain a variety of fruit juices mixed with ground chiles. Over the years, sangrita has evolved to derive its deep red color from tomato juice as opposed to chile powder. I personally prefer my sangrita as a blend of the old and the new, which is why this version includes both tomato juice and ground chiles. I like to mix sangrita in advance and refrigerate it for up to a day to allow the flavors to develop before serving it chilled in either lowball or shot glasses … with tequila blanco, of course!

16 ounces (2 cups) tomato juice

8 ounces (1 cup) freshly squeezed orange juice

8 ounces (1 cup) freshly squeezed lime juice

2 ounces (¼ cup) pomegranate juice

6 dashes hot sauce (a vinegar-based hot sauce works best here)

1 tablespoon ground ancho chile

pinch of salt

1 teaspoon freshly ground black pepper

Lemon slices for garnish (optional)

Combine all of the ingredients except for the lemon slices in a large pitcher and mix well. Add the lemon slices and refrigerate for at least 1 hour or up to 1 day before serving.

Note: I do not store or serve sangrita with ice as I prefer not to dilute its unique flavor. Instead, I serve my sangrita directly from the refrigerator and/or in chilled lowball or shot glasses. Be sure to stir your sangrita well before serving.

YIELD: 1 liter

tequila sunrise

1 tablespoon granulated white
   sugar

1 teaspoon lemon zest

ice

2 ounces (¼ cup) silver tequila

8 ounces (1 cup) freshly squeezed
   orange juice

2 dashes grenadine syrup

Maraschino cherry for garnish
   (optional)

This classic Arizona cocktail was conceived by a bartender at the iconic Arizona Biltmore Hotel. It is named for its visually stunning presentation of ombré sunrise shades and is almost too pretty to drink. Almost! This version carries the rainbow effect right up to the rim of the glass with a dusting of lemon sugar and is a perfectly beautiful way to end a hot summer day.

To prepare the lemon sugar, toss the sugar and lemon zest together in a small bowl and transfer to a saucer. Moisten the rim of a lowball glass and firmly press it into the lemon sugar until the rim is thoroughly coated.

Mix the ice, tequila, and orange juice together in a cocktail shaker and shake well. Pour into the prepared glass and then slowly add the grenadine without stirring, allowing it to sink to the bottom of the glass. Garnish and serve.

YIELD: 1 drink

cucumber & melon agua fresca

1 large (3 to 4 lb.) honeydew
    melon, peeled, seeded,
    coarsely chopped

2 large cucumbers, peeled,
    seeded, coarsely chopped*

½ cup granulated white sugar

ice

½ cup freshly squeezed lime
    juice

*I usually reserve half of one
of the cucumbers for garnish.
I simply retain the peel on that
piece, slice it horizontally into
rounds approximately ½-inch
thick, and set aside to add to
the finished drink. This step is
obviously optional.

special equipment: You will
need a finely woven cheesecloth or
fine mesh sieve to properly strain this
drink.

Agua frescas are a saving grace on hot summer days.
These 'fresh waters' come in a multitude of flavors and are
so thirst-quenching that I prefer to prepare them in large
batches to keep cool and on hand in the refrigerator. The
essences of cucumber and juicy honeydew melon make
this *agua fresca* particularly satisfying. Note that pitchers
of this drink also make for a pretty beverage offering at a
summer luncheon or fiesta.

....

Place the melon pieces, cucumber pieces, sugar, and 1
cup of water in the bowl of a food processor fitted with
a steel blade and process to a purée (you can work in
batches as needed).

Line a large colander with cheesecloth and set it over
a large bowl, or simply set your fine mesh sieve over
a large bowl. Pour the purée into the lined colander or
sieve and set aside to strain for approximately 1 hour.

After an hour, carefully gather the cheesecloth and
squeeze out any remaining juices, or agitate your sieve to
remove any residual juice. Discard the solids that remain.
Stir the melon and cucumber juice into a large pitcher
filled with ice. Stir in 7 cups water and the lime juice, and
garnish with cucumber rounds.

The flavor of this agua fresca gets even better if it is
allowed to sit and develop. This drink is also best serve
chilled; I opt to refrigerate my *agua fresca* instead of
adding ice in order to keep from diluting its flavor but you
may add ice if you prefer.

YIELD: approximately 2½ to 3 quarts

texas rose

This lovely Lone Star cocktail offers a fruity flavor and a refreshing crispness all in one sip. The ingredients come together to produce a drink that matches the color of a beautiful yellow rose in bloom. I like to garnish glasses of this cocktail with a pineapple wedge, just to give guests a hint of what's in store.

2 ounces (¼ cup) freshly squeezed orange juice

2 ounces (¼ cup) pineapple juice

1 ounce (2 tablespoons) crème de banane

1 ounce (2 tablespoons) light rum

½ ounce (1 tablespoon) freshly squeezed lime juice

ice

pineapple wedge for garnish (optional)

Mix the orange juice, pineapple juice, crème de banane, rum, and lime juice together in a cocktail shaker and shake well. Fill a lowball glass with ice and pour the mixed cocktail over top. Garnish and serve.

YIELD: 1 drink

appetizers & snacks

Snacks can often feel uninspired and utilitarian, so I like to keep a few exciting options in my bag of tricks. I love serving intriguing starters to guests and satisfying snacks to myself around three o'clock in the afternoon, which is why I take my small bites very seriously.

In the Southwest, many snacks and starters are based on *antojitos*, Mexican street food that is both served and consumed on the go. *Antojitos* need to be filling, flavorful, and quick, which is probably why they typically involve some sort of corn and/or corn-based *masa*. Southwestern starters are not all portable, but they do expand on the corn foundation to include other filling staples, such as beans and potatoes.

Because I usually find myself reaching for something hot when it comes to snack time or appetizers, you will find that each of the recipes included in this chapter, even the snack mix and salsa-soaked *chicharrones*, may be served warm. Alternatively, each of these small bites would work equally well set out on a buffet table at room temperature for a special occasion.

black bean & corn quesaditas

1 cup cooked black beans

1 cup cooked whole corn kernels

1 cup shredded Monterey Jack cheese

1 cup shredded Chihuahua cheese (mild cheddar may be substituted)

½ cup minced fresh chives

½ cup freshly squeezed lemon juice

1 tablespoon firmly packed dark brown sugar

1 teaspoon garlic powder

1 teaspoon salt

corn tortillas of any size large enough to cut out 3-inch rounds

1 teaspoon vegetable oil + more for frying

special equipment: You'll need a 3-inch cookie cutter to punch out the small shells for your *quesaditas*. I don't recommend making these *quesaditas* any smaller than 3 inches, as they become too difficult to stuff and fry. If you don't have a 3-inch cutter on hand, you can invert a coffee mug onto the tortillas and trace around the edge with a sharp knife to cut the shells out by hand. Obviously, I recommend that this, along with the frying, be done by an adult.

This teeny, tiny take on the quesadilla is perfect for assembling with and serving to kids. Preparation involves the simple work of tossing ingredients together and cutting out your tortilla shells. With help from a big friend, these small little snacks are fried to a crisp, the creamy melted cheese disguising healthy portions of black beans, corn, bright lemon, and chives. It's a win/win for big and small diners.

In a large bowl, toss together the black beans, corn, Monterey Jack and Chihuahua cheeses, and chives. In a separate small bowl, whisk together the lemon juice, brown sugar, garlic powder, and salt. Stir into the bean mixture.

Using a 3-inch cookie cutter, cut rounds out of the corn tortillas—you'll need between 40 and 44 tortilla circles. Place half of the circles on a rimmed baking sheet and top each with 2 tablespoons of the filling mixture. Top each with another tortilla circle.

Heat 1 teaspoon of oil in a large heavy-bottomed skillet over medium heat. Once the oil has heated, carefully transfer up to four quesaditas to the pan and fry for approximately 3 minutes, applying pressure to the tops of each as they cook. Carefully flip after 3 minutes and cook for an additional 3 to 4 minutes. Finished quesaditas will be crisped and golden brown, with their contents melted together.

Remove the cooked quesaditas to a baking sheet lined with paper towels to drain slightly before serving. Refresh your pan with an additional teaspoon of oil, and move on to the next batch of quesaditas. (I recommend refreshing your oil by the teaspoon in between each batch, and I do not recommend crowding your pan as you fry, mainly because the quesaditas will melt and ooze as they cook.) Serve with the salsa of your choosing stacking in tall stacks as shown if you prefer.

YIELD: approximately 20 to 22 quesaditas

salsa bandera chicharrones

Admittedly indulgent, yet sinfully difficult to resist, *chicharrones* (fried pork skins) are a snack of choice in the Southwest. I like to cut the richness of the rinds by serving them soaked in a warm restaurant-style salsa. The *chicharrones* are crispy and fatty, and the salsa is tart and bright—it's a match made in snacking heaven.

....

10 plum (Roma) tomatoes, ends removed, coarsely chopped

2 large jalapeños, stemmed, coarsely chopped

½ white onion, coarsely chopped

6 stems parsley, coarsely chopped

2 teaspoons ground white pepper

¼ cup freshly squeezed lime juice

1 3½-ounce bag chicharrones

Note: This recipe can easily be halved if you do not have a food processor with a big enough bowl or if you would simply like to prepare less salsa.

Place all the ingredients except the chicharrones in the bowl of a food processer fitted with a steel blade and process until smooth and uniform. Transfer to a large heavy-bottomed pot and bring to a boil. Reduce to a simmer and cook to marry flavors and reduce, stirring occasionally, approximately 20 minutes.

Meanwhile, spread chicharrones out onto a rimmed platter or large shallow bowl and set aside.

Once salsa has cooked and reduced down, remove from heat, immediately ladle over chicharrones, and serve.

YIELD: approximately 5 cups of salsa

not all chicharrones are created equal: While they are as ubiquitous as potato chips in Arizona, the small, snack-sized bags of *chicharrones* that you can find at gas stations are often loaded with artificial seasonings and preservatives. I recommend seeking out the best quality *chicharrón* that you can find for this dish. Take a moment to read the ingredients listed on the package, and be sure that you are getting only the fried pork skins seasoned with a bit of salt. It may seem like a bit of an oxymoron, but high-quality *chicharrones* make all the difference in this down and dirty snack.

spiced snack mix

1½ cups Spanish peanuts

1½ cups pepitas (dried pumpkin seeds), hulled

1 teaspoon ground ancho chile

1 teaspoon finely ground sea salt

1 teaspoon ground mustard

1 teaspoon ground cumin

1 teaspoon garlic powder

½ teaspoon ground oregano (preferably Mexican oregano)

½ teaspoon ground coriander

½ teaspoon ground white pepper

1 tablespoon extra virgin olive oil

Don't be deceived by this modest snack mix—there is nothing plain about its flavor. The distinctive red skin of Spanish peanuts absorbs a rainbow of seasonings, and the *pepitas* (dried pumpkin seeds) offer a unique crunch and textural alternative to the nuts. Ultimately, I believe that size not only matters when it comes to a snack mix, but it is the key to greatness. The matched size of the *pepitas* and tiny Spanish peanuts makes this mix infinitely consumable, and ultimately addictive.

....

Preheat oven to 300°F.

Toss the peanuts and pepitas together in a large bowl. Toss in the ancho, salt, ground mustard, cumin, garlic powder, oregano, coriander, and pepper, mixing until the nuts and pepitas are evenly and well coated in the seasonings. Once the seasoning is distributed, add the oil, again mixing until evenly and well coated.

Transfer the mixture to a rimmed baking sheet, spreading in an even layer. Toast for 20 minutes. Remove from oven and carefully toss. Toast for an additional 20 minutes, until mixture is dark golden brown and deeply fragrant. Remove from oven and set aside to cool slightly. Serve warm or store in a covered container for up to one week.

YIELD: approximately 3 cups

a note about tortillas

In their hurry to assemble the perfect taco, burrito, or *flauta*, people will often neglect to warm their tortillas before stuffing and manipulating into shape. Especially when working with smaller sizes as with these *flautas*, it is imperative to take a moment and warm your tortillas. Simply place the tortilla on a heated comal or dry fry pan and warm for 15 to 30 seconds on each side. Heating loosens the dough or *masa*, making your tortilla more pliable and much less likely to break apart as you stuff it full of goodies and bake, fry, or grill.

savory baked pumpkin flautas

1 tablespoon extra virgin olive oil + more for brushing

¾ cup diced yellow onion

1 tablespoon minced fresh garlic

2 cups pumpkin puree (canned or fresh)

1 teaspoon salt

1 teaspoon ground cumin

1 teaspoon freshly ground black pepper

2 tablespoons buttermilk

1½ cups shredded Oaxaca cheese (mozzarella cheese may be substituted)

12 or 13 small (5- to 6-inch) flour tortillas

Flautas, stuffed rolled tortillas named for the musical instrument that they most closely resemble, are usually pan-fried or deep-fried. This lightened-up version is oven-baked but doesn't skimp on rich flavor. Sweet pumpkin is paired with caramelized onions and creamy Oaxaca cheese, and stuffed inside flour tortillas for a savory twist on a classic squash taste. Baked until crisp, melty, and irresistible, these *flautas* make perfect snacks or starters.

Preheat oven to 425°F.

Heat the oil in a large, heavy-bottomed skillet over low-medium heat. Add the onion and sauté slowly. The onion will slowly go from translucent, lightly colored, to deep golden brown, approximately 10 minutes. Once the onion is browned, add the garlic and cook for 2 minutes more. Set aside to cool slightly.

Meanwhile, place the pumpkin, salt, cumin, black pepper, buttermilk, and shredded cheese in a large bowl and stir until well-blended. Fold in the cooled onion mixture.

Warm the tortillas and place on a flat surface to assemble. Top each tortilla with just 2 to 3 tablespoons of the pumpkin mixture, roll tightly into a cigar shape, and place, seam-side down, on a parchment-lined baking sheet.

Brush the top of each flauta lightly with oil and bake for approximately 20 minutes or until the flautas are golden brown on top and the tortillas are crisped. Cool slightly before serving.

YIELD: 12 or 13 flautas

sweet potato & bacon sopes

Sopes are thick, fried *masa* cakes topped with the savory stuff of your choosing. These hearty *sopes* carry one of my favorite combinations: mashed sweet potatoes, caramelized onions, and salty crisp bacon. While you may opt to form your *masa* into smaller, bite-sized *sopes*, I prefer mine on the larger side. All the better for conveying a maximum amount of the irresistible topping.

....

For the sopes:

3 cups masa harina

1 teaspoon salt

2½ cups warm water

¼ cup canola oil for frying

For the topping:

1 tablespoon extra virgin olive oil

½ cup diced yellow onion

2 teaspoons minced fresh garlic

2 cups sweet potato purée

1 teaspoon ground cumin

¾ teaspoon ground ancho chile

½ teaspoon salt

1 cup crumbled crisp cooked bacon

minced cilantro for garnish (optional)

To prepare the sopes, place masa harina and salt in a large bowl and slowly pour in the warm water. Stir the mixture with a fork for several seconds and then switch to clean hands as the dough begins to come together into a ball. The dough will be quite dry but should still hold the shape of a ball. If not, you may add more warm water, up to ½ cup, until the dough is moist enough to hold shape. Knead the dough several times and cover with a damp cloth. Set aside to rest for 30 minutes.

After the resting period, heat a dry large heavy-bottomed skillet over medium-high heat. Pinch off plum-size pieces of dough and flatten to a thickness of approximately ½ inch. Have a piece of parchment paper and a glass or other small vessel with a bottom diameter slightly smaller than that of your sopes on hand in order to finish shaping the cakes. Add a sope to the dry skillet and cook for just 1 minute on each side. Remove and immediately press down with your glass with a piece of parchment paper in between; the idea is to form a rim on your sope so that it can better hold your topping. Set aside the warm formed sope and repeat with the remaining masa.

Once all of your sopes have been formed, add the canola oil to the pan and warm over medium heat. Working in batches, add the formed sopes and fry until golden, just 4 to 5 minutes on each side. Remove to a paper towel-lined surface to drain and cool.

Meanwhile, to prepare the topping, heat the olive oil in a large heavy-bottomed skillet over medium heat. Add the onion and sauté, stirring frequently, until tender, fragrant, and translucent, approximately 5 minutes. Add the garlic and sauté for just 2 minutes more. Remove and set aside to cool. Place the sweet potato purée in a large bowl and stir in the cumin, ancho, salt, and bacon. Stir in the cooked onion and garlic.

Top each fried sope generously with the sweet potato mixture, garnish with cilantro and serve immediately.

YIELD: approximately 10 to 12 sopes

breads

Bread—in all varieties—is a well-considered addition to any feast. I know that when I am served a meal that includes a stocked, steaming bread basket I always feel that the host or hostess has put some serious thought into the meal. I like to return the favor by serving freshly baked bread as often as possible. And since tortillas, biscuits, and rolls can also form the foundation for a memorable taco or sandwich, I'll always have some of each on hand in my kitchen.

Beyond simply serving and consuming it, assembling and baking traditional breads plays a critical role in daily life and on special occasions on Native American reservations throughout the Southwest. As a result, crusty yeasted loaves, blue corn-based tortillas, and even fried fritters have long been a part of Southwestern cuisine.

Because baking was what originally brought me into the kitchen as an adult, I truly relish the process of assembling, handling, and shaping dough into a finished product that is so much more satisfying than the store-bought alternative. I think you'll find that the following breads are as enjoyable to produce as they are to snack on and share. Be sure to store your breads carefully, as most will keep for days when wrapped tightly and kept cool and dry.

hopi blue corn tortillas

1½ cups blue cornmeal

½ cup all-purpose flour + more
for dusting

2 cups boiling water

Blue corn was originally cultivated by the Hopi people and remains an integral part of their culinary and ceremonial way of life. Whether ground to a meal or used as whole kernels, blue corn lends a particularly nutty flavor to stews and breads and, of course, a brilliant violet hue to finished dishes. These tortillas make a lovely addition to any meal, an intriguing alternative to standard yellow and white corn tortillas, and are perfectly delicious when piled high with the vegetable and meat toppings of your choosing.

....

Whisk the blue cornmeal and flour together in a large bowl. Using a wooden spoon, carefully stir in the boiling water. Once the dough has come together, set it aside to rest for 5 minutes.

Flour your hands and a large, flat work surface. Remove the dough to the prepared work surface and knead for 1 to 2 minutes, replenishing the flour on your hands and the surface as needed. Divide the dough into 8 balls and dust the tops of each with flour.

hopi blue corn: The Hopi have been farming a wide variety of corn for over one thousand years, and are in fact responsible for the development of a number of those varieties. Blue corn, in particular, also known as Hopi maize, has been highly cultivated over the years by the Hopi people. Single farms will grow multiple types of blue corn, and will adapt new and existing varieties to produce the heartiest most pest-resistant crop possible. While most people outside of the reservation know Hopi blue corn for its use in traditional piki bread, the corn also plays an important role in tribal ceremonies and special occasions.

Heat a comal or dry pan over medium heat. Once the pan is hot, pat a ball of dough into a 3-inch round disc. Place the dough disc on the hot pan and immediately flatten using a wooden spatula. You will want to press outwards from the center of the tortilla, quickly spreading the dough to double its original 3-inch size. Cook for at least 2 minutes on each side; the tortilla is done when dark brown spots begin to appear on its surface. Remove from skillet and repeat with remaining dough.

These tortillas are best enjoyed right out of the pan, but you may store them in a covered container and reheat for later use.

YIELD: Eight 6-inch tortillas

cheesy beer bread

3 cups all-purpose flour

2 teaspoons baking powder

1 teaspoon baking soda

1 teaspoon salt

1 cup buttermilk

1 cup vegetable oil

1 cup beer (preferably dark Mexican lager or other dark beer)

2 cups shredded sharp white cheddar cheese

A crusty loaf of bread flavored with sharp cheese and rich dark beer is always a hit for rounding out a meal or delivering to a man cave near you. Slice off a thick piece and use it to sop up the rest of your green chile stew, or simply toast and top with butter in the morning or at snack time. Even as flavorful bookends for a sandwich, you'll find this bread to be quite versatile, and quite in demand. I recommend shredding the cheese right off of the block; sharp white cheddar has a lovely bite that works perfectly in this bread, and shredding by hand ensures maximum and even melting.

Position a rack in the center of the oven, removing any higher racks, and preheat oven to 350°F.

Line the bottom of a 9x5x3-inch loaf pan with parchment paper, coat the sides with cooking spray and set aside.

Whisk the flour, baking powder, baking soda, and salt together in a large bowl. Slowly beat in the buttermilk, vegetable oil, and beer. Fold in the cheese. Place the dough in the prepared pan and smooth the top, finishing with a vertical slash down the top of the loaf to allow for even rising.

Bake for 45 to 50 minutes or until the loaf is puffed and golden brown on the top, the edges are peeling away slightly from the pan, and the bread is baked through. Allow the loaf to cool for approximately 10 minutes before removing from pan.

YIELD: One 9x5-inch loaf

sage & honey skillet biscuits

3½ cups all-purpose flour

3¼ teaspoons baking soda

2 teaspoons ground sage

1 teaspoon salt

¾ teaspoon ground white pepper

¼ cup unsalted butter, chilled
    and cubed, plus some melted
    butter for greasing the pan
    and finishing the biscuits

2 cups buttermilk

1 cup honey

melted butter for finishing

Sage and honey, two iconic flavors of the Southwest, pair perfectly together here in buttery, light biscuits baked directly in a cast-iron skillet. This dense, moist bread is flavorful enough to be enjoyed on its own, yet mild enough to play the part of a starchy, satisfying side dish in any spread. I love serving these biscuits directly out of the pan in which they are baked. The rustic presentation always seems to delight, and the piping hot biscuits carry the ever so slight flavor of well-seasoned cast iron.

Preheat oven to 475°F.

Grease a 10-inch cast-iron skillet with some melted butter and set aside.

Place the flour, baking soda, sage, salt, and white pepper in the bowl of a food processor fitted with a steel blade and pulse-process just to blend. Add the chilled butter to the flour mixture and process until a coarse meal forms.

Pour the flour mixture into a large bowl and mix in the buttermilk and honey—I recommend simply using clean hands to mix; you want to ensure that all of the ingredients are incorporated without overworking your dough and you also want to move as quickly as possible to be sure that the warmth from your hands doesn't melt the bits of butter in the dough.

Once the mixture is uniform, divide the dough into 10 small balls and place them in a ring around the edge of the prepared pan. Place 2 final balls of dough in the center of the pan. (No need to flatten the balls of dough.) Yielding exactly 10 biscuits is not absolutely necessary here; you can also fit 9 or 11 biscuits in your pan. The edges of the unbaked biscuits may be touching inside the pan.

Place the filled pan in the oven and bake for approximately 15 minutes. Remove pan from the oven, brush the tops of the biscuits generously with melted butter, and bake for an additional 3 to 5 minutes. Cool slightly or serve immediately.

YIELD: approximately 10 biscuits

pueblo bread

1 packet (¼ ounce) dry active yeast

1 teaspoon granulated white sugar

1¼ cups warm water (100°F to 110°F), divided

¼ cup honey

½ tablespoon vegetable shortening, melted

1 teaspoon salt

3 cups all-purpose flour, plus more for dusting your work surface

These crusty, rustic loaves have been prepared by the Pueblo Indians of New Mexico for generations. The bread is baked in extremely large community batches in stone *hornos* built from New Mexican clay soil. The dough is assembled a day before baking and set aside to rise in large washtubs or basins. The day of baking, loaves are formed and baked over fires made from fragrant local piñon wood; the entire process is as much a ritual as it is a production line with a delicious finished product. The yield is a crusty white bread, not dissimilar from traditional European white breads. This recipe has obviously been adapted to accommodate conventional ovens and produces two hearty loaves. Eat warm from the oven slathered with butter or store sealed to use for sandwiches and toast. Either way, this bread is likely to become a staple in your household.

....

Preheat oven to 350°F.

Dissolve yeast and sugar in a small bowl with ¼ cup of the warm water. Set aside to bloom for 5 to 10 minutes.

Meanwhile, mix the remaining 1 cup warm water, honey, melted shortening, and salt together in the bowl of a stand mixer fitted with a paddle attachment, or whisk together in a large bowl. Once yeast has bloomed, carefully mix or whisk the yeast mixture into the honey mixture, blending until just combined.

Mix or whisk in the flour, 1 cup at a time, mixing or whisking well after each addition, until you have a cohesive mass of dough. At this point, switch to the dough hook if working with a stand mixer, or transfer the dough to a well-floured work surface if working by hand.

special equipment:

I recommend using a stand mixer to prepare this bread; the machinery cuts down on the elbow grease you must exert, and actually yields a smoother, more elastic dough with a lighter crumb in the finished loaves. I have, however, included directions for both electronic and hand methods.

Use your dough hook or hands to knead the dough until smooth and elastic, approximately 3 to 5 minutes in a stand mixer or 6 to 8 minutes by hand. Divide kneaded dough in half and shape into oblong loaves by tucking and rolling the edges up and underneath. Set both loaves on a parchment-lined baking sheet, cover with a damp towel and set aside in a warm area of your kitchen to rise and double in volume, approximately 60 to 90 minutes (keep in mind that this time can vary depending on the conditions in your kitchen).

Once bread has risen, preheat the oven to 350°F. Slash both loaves across the top with a large 'X' to allow for even rising and bake on the parchment-lined baking sheet for 40 to 50 minutes or until the bread is cooked through. Finished loaves will be deep golden brown, crusted and firm on the surface. Slice and serve immediately or store, sealed for up to one week.

YIELD: Two 1-pound loaves

vinegar biscuits

2 cups all-purpose flour plus more for dusting

1 tablespoon baking powder

¼ teaspoon baking soda

1 teaspoon salt

3 tablespoons unsalted butter, chilled, cubed

3 teaspoons vegetable shortening

¾ cup chilled buttermilk

¼ cup distilled white vinegar

These fluffy, layered biscuits take their cue from the days of the chuckwagon, when flavor agents were scarce and prohibitively expensive, and vinegar was often used in their stead. It may seem odd to bake simple distilled white vinegar into these light little rolls, but the vinegar actually works in tandem with fresh buttermilk to produce an extremely moist biscuit that pairs well with just about any main course, be it breakfast, lunch, or dinner.

• •

Note: The key to yielding the best biscuit here has everything to do with the way you handle the dough. Actually, it has most to do with how little you handle the dough. I strongly recommend cutting your butter and shortening in by hand, eschewing a rolling pin, and pushing your cutter straight down without twisting so as to avoid sealing the edges of each biscuit and preventing a complete rise.

Preheat oven to 450°F.

Whisk the flour, baking powder, baking soda, and salt together in a large bowl. Working as quickly as possible and using clean hands, cut the chilled butter and vegetable shortening into the dry ingredients, mixing the fats into the flour mixture until you have a coarse, chunky meal. Pour in the buttermilk and vinegar, and again using clean hands, mix the ingredients together until you have a solid mass of dough.

Turn the dough out onto a lightly floured work surface and pat into a flat disk approximately ½-inch thick. Using a 3-inch cutter, press straight down into the dough to cut out each biscuit (keep your cutting as tight as possible in order to minimize scraps). Remove cut biscuits to a parchment-lined baking sheet—I find that these biscuits bake better when they are arranged in rows with their edges just touching each other. Pat remaining scraps together and cut out additional biscuits. Once all biscuits have been cut out, bake for approximately 12 to 15 minutes, until they are puffed and golden brown on the tops and bottoms. Remove from oven and serve immediately.

YIELD: approximately 12 biscuits

the three sisters—squash, corn or maize, and climbing beans—are a seminal example of agricultural symbiosis in the Americas. Corn stalks provide an infrastructure on which beans can grow; bean vines infuse life-giving nitrogen into the soil; and squash plants spread across the ground preventing the infiltration of weeds. In culinary terms, the three sisters are one of the original examples of 'what grows together goes together'; beans, corn, and squash, when consumed as a single dish, produce a wonderful form of flavor alchemy. Although the 'bean' sister is usually represented by a variety of climbing bean, this recipe uses black beans to equally delicious results.

three sisters hush puppies

1½ cups yellow cornmeal

½ cup all-purpose flour

2¼ teaspoons baking powder

1 teaspoon salt

1 teaspoon ground white pepper

2 eggs, lightly beaten

1 cup buttermilk

¼ cup diced yellow onion

½ cup cooked black beans

½ cup cooked whole corn
    kernels

½ cup grated zucchini

6 cups peanut oil for frying

Hush puppies have been around for much longer than most people realize. The process of grinding or pounding dried, hardened kernels of corn into a meal originated with the ancient Aztec and Mayan cultures and was later adopted by a number of Native American tribes. It is fitting, therefore, that this version is stuffed with a combination coined by Native Americans as the "three sisters": squash, corn, and beans. These hearty little fried breads are extremely difficult to resist, especially when paired with a cream sauce such as Roasted Crema (page 54), and when served straight out of the fryer.

Whisk the cornmeal, flour, baking powder, salt, and pepper together in a large bowl. Whisk in the eggs and buttermilk until you have a smooth, uniform batter. Fold in the onion, beans, corn, and zucchini.

Heat the oil in a large heavy-bottomed pot to a frying temperature of 350° to 365°F. Drop the batter by heaping tablespoons into the hot oil. (I strongly recommend cleaning your teaspoon and wetting it lightly with water or cool peanut oil in between scoops of batter, as well as taking care not to overcrowd your pan.) Fry the hush puppies until golden brown and cooked through, turning while they cook, approximately 3 to 4 minutes. Remove to a paper towel-lined baking sheet to drain slightly and serve.

You may wish to keep the cooked hush puppies in an oven preheated to 250°F while you finish frying, as you will almost certainly need to work in batches.

YIELD: approximately 6 to 8 servings

side dishes

I love a good side dish—who doesn't? There's just something so comforting about a cheesy steaming dish of potatoes, a well-flavored pot of rice, or a bowl of freshly seasoned and sautéed vegetables.

Southwestern cuisine includes a number of basic indigenous ingredients that are simply made for serving on the side, namely beans, corn, and rice. When it comes to these hearty staples, I really like to punch up the flavor. As a result, you'll find the recipes in this chapter include dishes such as tequila-spiked beans, cheesy corn pudding, and tart rice electrified by the addition of fresh citrus juice and roasted chiles. Just because it's on the side, doesn't mean it shouldn't still be interesting! Which is probably why you'll find, just as I do when I serve these sides, that they're often the first part of the meal to go.

adobo potato gratin

3 large garlic cloves

extra virgin olive oil for roasting

pinch of salt for roasting

4 chipotle chiles in adobo sauce

1¼ cups heavy cream

¾ cup whole milk

4 tablespoons unsalted butter

1 teaspoon freshly ground black
  pepper

3 large Russet potatoes, peeled,
  ends removed, cut into
  ⅛-inch-thick slices

1¾ cups shredded Chihuahua
  cheese, divided (medium
  sharp cheddar cheese may
  be substituted)

special equipment: If you have
one on hand, I strongly recommend
using a mandolin to slice the
potatoes in this recipe. Producing
potato slices of uniform thickness just
means that your gratin will bake more
evenly, and the mandolin makes this
task a snap.

This gratin really does bring all the boys to the yard. It's
rich, it's creamy, it's cheesy, and while baking, it produces
an unbelievably luxurious aroma that will perfume your
entire kitchen in the best way possible. The kicker?
This casserole is incredibly simple to prepare, and can
be assembled ahead of time, refrigerated, and baked
whenever you're ready to enjoy. And bring all the boys to
your yard.

Preheat oven to 350°F.

Toss the garlic cloves with the oil and salt, wrap tightly in
a foil packet, and roast for approximately 30 minutes or
until fragrant and golden brown. Remove from oven and
increase oven temperature to 400°F.

Place roasted garlic in the bowl of a food processer
fitted with a steel blade along with the whole chipotle
chiles. Process to a paste. Put the garlic-chile paste
in a large heavy-bottomed skillet and add cream, milk,
butter, and pepper. Cooking over medium heat and
stirring frequently, bring mixture to a boil and boil for just
1 minute to thicken. Remove from heat and set aside to
cool slightly.

Layer half of the potato slices in an overlapping pattern
in the bottom of a 2-quart baking dish. Top with a light
sprinkle of cheese and repeat with the remaining potato
slices and 1 cup of the cheese. Carefully pour the cream
mixture over top of the potato layers. You may need to
agitate your dish slightly, just to be sure that everything
settles and the cream gets into as many nooks and
crannies as possible. Sprinkle the remaining cheese as
evenly as possible over the top layer of potatoes.

Bake for approximately 40 to 50 minutes, or until the casserole is deep golden brown and bubbling on top, and the potatoes are fork tender and cooked through. Remove baked gratin from oven and set aside to cool slightly before serving.

YIELD: approximately 6 to 8 servings

chipotle twice-baked sweet potatoes

½ cup walnuts, coarsely chopped

4 large sweet potatoes*

¼ cup unsalted butter, melted

¼ cup firmly packed light brown sugar

1 tablespoon ground chipotle chile

1 teaspoon ground ancho chile

1 teaspoon ground canela (ground cinnamon may be substituted)

salt to taste

½ cup golden raisins

extra virgin olive oil

*Note: As sweet potatoes can often vary significantly in shape and size, it is worth it when purchasing for this recipe to take care and select sweet potatoes that are as evenly rounded and similarly sized as possible. You should also take a moment before baking to set them flat on your work surface and be sure that you are baking them right side up, that is, the side on which the potato wants to rest is facing down.

Sweet potatoes are the perfect candidate for twice-baking. Softening and caramelizing their exteriors, mixing their flesh with brown sugar, plump golden raisins, and a hint of warm canela and smoky chipotle, and tossing in a handful of crunchy, toasted walnuts yields a hearty side dish that's welcome anytime. These lovely sweet potatoes go wonderfully with just about any main course, but I especially love to serve them with pork or lamb chops straight from the grill or stovetop pan.

....

Preheat oven to 375°F.

Spread walnut pieces evenly on a rimmed baking sheet and toast until fragrant and light golden brown, 5 to 7 minutes. Remove from oven and set aside to cool.

Meanwhile, pierce the tops of each potato several times with a fork, place on a rimmed baking sheet and bake until tender, approximately 60 to 75 minutes. Set aside to cool.

Once the potatoes are cool enough to handle, split the tops of each and carefully scoop the flesh out to a large bowl, reserving the skins. Stir the butter, brown sugar, chipotle, ancho, and canela into the potato flesh, mixing just until you have a smooth, uniform purée. Season with salt to taste. Fold in the toasted walnut pieces and raisins.

Carefully refill the potato skins with the mixture and top each with a light drizzle of olive oil. Return to the oven and bake for 10 to 15 minutes or until the tops are golden brown. Serve immediately.

YIELD: 4 servings

skillet-baked corn pudding

4 cups canned or cooked fresh
    whole corn kernels, divided

4 jalapeños, roasted, peeled,
    stemmed, and seeded

1 tablespoon extra virgin olive oil

½ cup diced yellow onion

2 teaspoons minced fresh garlic

5 large eggs

1 cup whole milk

1 cup all-purpose flour

1½ teaspoons baking powder

1 teaspoon salt

1 cup shredded Monterey Jack
    cheese

It's hard to imagine a more comforting dish than corn pudding, and this creamy, colorful version does not disappoint. Roasted jalapeños add just the right amount of heat, melted Monterey Jack cheese brings the richness, and five whole eggs yield a soufflé-like consistency that goes way beyond tempting. This savory pudding is satisfying enough to serve as a vegetarian main course or a hearty side.

....

Preheat oven to 450°F.

Place 2 cups of corn and the prepared jalapeños in the bowl of a food processor fitted with a steel blade and puree. Set aside.

Heat the olive oil in a large 3½ quart oven-proof skillet. Add the onion and sauté until fragrant and translucent, approximately 5 minutes. Add the garlic and sauté for 2 more minutes. Stir in the pureed corn mixture and cook for approximately 4 more minutes, then remove from heat.

Whisk the eggs in a large bowl. Whisk in the milk, flour, baking powder, and salt, mixing just until you have a smooth, uniform batter. Fold in the remaining 2 cups corn and the cheese.

Stir the batter mixture into the sautéd mixture in the skillet, mixing well to blend all ingredients. Carefully transfer the filled skillet to the oven and bake for 25 to 30 minutes or until the top of the pudding is golden brown and set. Serve immediately.

YIELD: approximately 6 servings

pecan-crusted baked rice

2 cups whole pecans

3 tablespoons extra virgin olive oil, divided

1 teaspoon freshly ground black pepper

2 cups long-grain white rice

1½ cups diced yellow onion

3 tablespoons minced fresh garlic

2 teaspoons ground cumin

4 cups vegetable stock

salt to taste

2 cups shredded Manchego cheese, divided

Rice and nuts make natural bedfellows—it's the perfect match of crunch and cushion. Add in a hefty dose of creamy, nutty Manchego cheese, and you've got a baked rice casserole that is as satisfying as it is delicious.

Preheat oven to 350°F.

Toss pecans with 1 tablespoon of the olive oil and the black pepper, spread in an even layer on a baking sheet and toast until dark golden brown and fragrant, approximately 8 minutes. Remove from oven and set aside to cool. Once cool enough to handle, coarsely chop and set aside again.

Increase the oven temperature to 400°F.

Heat remaining 2 tablespoons of olive oil over medium heat in a heavy-bottomed skillet. Add the rice and onion and sauté for approximately 5 minutes, or until rice grains are opaque and onion is translucent and tender. Add the garlic and sauté for just 2 to 3 minutes more. Stir in the cumin and stock, season with salt to taste, bring to a boil, and reduce to a simmer. Cover and cook until moisture is absorbed and rice is tender, approximately 20 minutes. Remove pan from heat and transfer rice to a large, heat-proof bowl.

Toss the cooked rice with 1½ cups of the cheese and 1 cup of the nut pieces, and transfer the mixture to a 2-quart baking dish. Top with remaining cheese and nut pieces. Bake for approximately 20 minutes or until cheese is melted and the top of the casserole is crusted and golden brown. You may opt to broil your rice for an additional 1 to 2 minutes, just to really crisp up the crust on top. Remove from oven and serve immediately.

YIELD: approximately 6 servings

drunken black beans

Having a fantastic scratch bean recipe in your back pocket is like owning a quality wristwatch: you'll be happy to have it on hand when you need it, and it will serve you well for the rest of your life. These black beans can round out just about any meal, top virtually any taco, and finish off a burrito of any size. This recipe yields quite a bit of beans, which means you can serve a crowd or keep them in your refrigerator to use as needed. Now if only we could get these beans to tell us the time …

1½ pounds dried black beans, picked over for stones or foreign objects and rinsed

2 tablespoons extra virgin olive oil

1 large yellow onion, diced

3 large jalapeños, minced

2 tablespoons minced fresh garlic

¼ cup tequila (I recommend using either a reposado or añejo tequila here)

Place the beans in a large bowl and add enough water to cover them by at least 2 inches. Cover and set aside to soak overnight.

Drain soaked beans. Place beans in a large stockpot and again add enough water to cover by at least 2 inches. Bring to a boil, skimming off any foam that forms at the top of the pot, reduce to a simmer, cover and cook until beans are tender, approximately 90 to 105 minutes. Remove cooked beans from heat, drain and set aside to cool slightly.

Meanwhile, in the same stockpot, heat the olive oil over medium heat. Add the onion and jalapeños and sauté until tender, approximately 5 to 7 minutes. Add the garlic and sauté for 2 more minutes. Stir in the beans, then carefully stir in the tequila. Once the ingredients are all mixed together, mash the beans with a potato masher to a chunky consistency. The finished texture of these beans is important—I do not recommend using a stick blender or any other mechanical device to mash. I have found that good old elbow grease and a hand-held potato masher yields the best results.

Serve right away or store, covered, for up to 2 weeks.

YIELD: approximately 8 to 9 cups of beans

fried sage smashed potatoes

Smashed red-skin potatoes are just so comforting and satisfying—how could they get any better? Perhaps by stirring in some delicately fried sage leaves? Perhaps. Perhaps by adding a hefty dose of butter, garlic, and rich, creamy ricotta cheese? Perhaps. Perhaps this recipe is destined to become a family favorite and instant classic in your household? For sure.

1½ pounds small red potatoes

2 cups peanut oil*

6 large sage leaves

½ cup ricotta cheese

¼ cup buttermilk

2 tablespoons butter, melted

2 teaspoons garlic powder

salt to taste

freshly ground black pepper to taste

¼ cup chopped parsley

*Canola or vegetable oil may be substituted here, but I find that, especially when working with ingredients as delicate as sage leaves, peanut oil is the best for heating and frying evenly.

Place the potatoes in a heavy-bottomed stockpot with enough water to cover. Bring the water to a boil and cook until potatoes are fork-tender, approximately 20 to 30 minutes. Drain the potatoes in a large colander and set aside to cool slightly.

Meanwhile, heat the peanut oil over high heat in a large heavy-bottomed pan. Once the oil is shimmering, add the sage leaves (the leaves should bubble immediately on contact with the oil) and fry until crispy, approximately 10 to 15 seconds. Carefully remove the fried leaves with a slotted spoon and place on a papertowel-lined surface to drain.

While the sage leaves drain, stir the ricotta cheese, buttermilk, butter, and garlic powder together in a medium bowl and set aside.

Place the cooled cooked potatoes in a large bowl and using a potato masher smash to a chunky consistency, taking care not to overwork your potatoes. Once the potatoes have been smashed but are still quite chunky, stir in the ricotta mixture. Season with salt and pepper to taste, then crumble the fried sage leaves over top, add the parsley and gently fold into the potatoes. Serve immediately.

YIELD: approximately 4 to 6 servings

savory corn cakes

These simple griddle cakes are a year-round staple in my household—they're just so versatile and easy to prepare. I use fresh sweet corn when it's in season, but do not hesitate to substitute frozen (thawed) kernels when it's not. Either way, these light, fluffy corn cakes will serve you well as a savory side dish, energizing breakfast, or even a hearty snack.

....

Whisk the flour, baking powder, and salt together in a large bowl.

In a separate bowl, whisk the milk, sour cream, and egg together. Whisk the wet ingredients into the dry ingredients, mixing just until you have a smooth, uniform batter. Fold in the corn and green onions.

Heat 1 tablespoon oil in a heavy-bottomed skillet over medium heat (assuming you will be frying these corn cakes in batches, I recommend adding approximately 1 tablespoon of oil to your pan before cooking each batch). Using ¼-cup measure, portion out 3 or 4 corn cakes into the skillet. Fry corn cakes for approximately 3 minutes on the first side, until air holes appear across the top of each corn cake, and their shapes are set and matte colored. Flip and cook 3 to 4 more minutes, until corn cakes are cooked through. Serve immediately. Continue cooking batches of corn cakes until all the batter is used.

YIELD: 12 to 14 corn cakes

1 cup all-purpose flour

1 teaspoon baking powder

1 teaspoon salt

¾ cup whole milk

½ cup sour cream

1 large egg

2½ cups canned or cooked fresh whole corn kernels

1 cup diced green onions

vegetable oil for frying

arroz verde

❧ green rice ☙

I love a good sticky rice. And I love a good flavorful, veggie-laced rice. Luckily, this green rice is an effective multitasker. Using a starchy, medium-grain rice yields a creamy finished texture, and a spicy purée of roasted chiles and herbs keeps things fresh and bright. *Arroz verde* pairs well with anything from fish to grilled pork, and is absolutely heavenly stuffed inside a burrito.

....

3 large shallots, peeled and ends removed

4 large cloves garlic

3 tablespoons extra virgin olive oil, divided

salt for roasting and seasoning to taste

3 poblano chiles, roasted, peeled, stemmed, and seeded

6 stems parsley

3 tablespoons freshly squeezed lime juice

2 cups medium-grain rice, such as Calrose or Indian Basmati

4 cups vegetable stock

Preheat oven to 350°F.

Toss the shallots and garlic together with 1 tablespoon of the oil and a pinch of salt, wrap tightly in foil and roast for approximately 50 minutes or until shallots are slightly shrunken and garlic is golden and fragrant. Place in the bowl of a food processor fitted with a steel blade. Add the poblano chiles, parsley, and lime juice and process to a uniform paste.

Heat the remaining 2 tablespoons of oil over medium heat. Add the rice and cook for 3 to 4 minutes, stirring occasionally, until the grains are opaque. Add the processed chile mixture and cook for an additional 3 to 4 minutes. Stir in the stock, season with salt to taste, and bring to a boil. Reduce heat to low, cover, and cook for 20 to 25 minutes or until all of the moisture has been absorbed and rice is tender. Fluff and stir before serving.

YIELD: approximately 6 servings

carrots baked in cream

1 pound carrots, peeled, halved vertically

2 tablespoons firmly packed light brown sugar

1 teaspoon ground canela (cinnamon may be substituted)

1 teaspoon salt

½ teaspoon ground nutmeg

½ teaspoon ground ancho chile

1 cup heavy cream

I love serving this simple side dish with grilled meat or spicy main courses—naturally sweet carrots are the perfect way to round out a smoky hot meal. Baked in rich cream, the carrots become impossibly tender and absorb the flavor of the cinnamon and nutmeg. Plus, this dish couldn't be easier to assemble and cook. You can double or even triple the recipe to feed a carrot-loving crowd.

Preheat oven to 350°F.

Spread carrot halves out in an even layer in a 2 qt. baking dish.

Whisk brown sugar, canela, salt, nutmeg, and ancho together in a small bowl. Whisk in the cream. Pour seasoned cream over carrots and toss to coat.

Cover baking dish tightly with foil and bake for approximately 60 minutes, until carrots are fork tender and fragrant. Remove baked carrots to a separate serving dish, top with several tablespoons of the cooking liquid (discarding the remainder), and serve immediately.

YIELD: approximately 6 servings

main courses

When I talk about Southwestern cuisine with people from other parts of the country or the world, there are certain things that I hear over and over: Tacos!, Burritos!, Enchiladas!, Quesadillas!. Yes, it's true, many Southwestern meals are based on these staple dishes, but they involve so much more flavor and freshness than most people suspect. Because of the expansion of the Southwestern pantry, classic dishes have evolved into modern riffs that render traditional staples virtually unrecognizable in the best way possible. Tacos now include roasted root vegetables and cumin-spiced hummus, enchiladas go vertical with the help of fresh local squash, and quesadillas get their indulgent creaminess from a hefty dose of fried avocado cut with a sweet *pico de gallo*. That's what reinvention is all about!

This chapter includes meat-based dishes along with vegetarian and vegan options as well. Note that each of these recipes is designed to be prepared inside your kitchen: see the next chapter for options to be cooked outside on the grill.

fideo burritos

¼ cup extra virgin olive oil

1 (12 ounce) package cut fideo (broken angel hair pasta may be substituted)

¾ cup diced yellow onion

2 cups diced plum (Roma) tomatoes (ends removed)

6 chipotle chiles in adobo sauce, diced

2 tablespoons minced fresh garlic

4 cups vegetable broth

1 teaspoon ground oregano (preferably Mexican oregano)

1 teaspoon ground cumin

1½ cups finely grated cotija añejo cheese (finely grated Parmesan cheese may be substituted)

salt to taste*

8 large burrito-size flour tortillas (approximately 12 inches in diameter)

*Both the broth and cotija cheese have a tendency to be extremely salty, so be sure to taste carefully before adding additional salt.

Burritos have gotten a bad rap these days, most likely because they've devolved into greasy, tree trunk-sized monstrosities. It's ironic that they are most commonly known by their diminutive moniker, which translates to "little donkey," as opposed to simply *burros*. I think it's time to give burritos a second chance, and I'm starting the intervention here by stuffing them with lightly sautéed, extraordinarily flavorful fideo pasta. Fideo pasta is most commonly sold 'cut' or 'coiled' and is generally used in soups or casseroles; this version keeps things portable by wrapping the cut pasta in warm flour tortillas, but not before tossing with a generous sprinkle of salty cotija cheese. All hail the new and improved burrito!

Warm the oil in a large, heavy-bottomed skillet over medium heat. Add the fideo and onion, and sauté until the pasta pieces have begun to brown and the onion pieces are fragrant and translucent, approximately 5 to 7 minutes.

Add the tomatoes, chiles, and garlic, and sauté for approximately 4 more minutes, stirring often to incorporate the ingredients. Stir in the broth, oregano, and cumin, and bring the mixture to a boil. Cover, reduce to a simmer, and continue to cook until the pasta is tender and the liquid has reduced, approximately 10 to 12 minutes.

Remove cooked pasta to a large, heat-proof bowl and immediately toss with the cheese (heatproof tongs come in really handy when finishing this pasta and assembling your burritos). Taste for salt and add a little if needed.

Meanwhile, warm the tortillas on a large comal or in a dry pan, and place on a flat surface to begin assembling.

Place ¾ to 1 cup of the pasta mixture in the center of a warmed tortilla. Fold the bottom of the tortilla (the edge closest to you) up and over the filling, then fold each side in and over the bottom. Tightly tuck and roll the burrito away from you to finish. Repeat with remaining tortillas. These burritos are best served immediately but you can also prepare the pasta filling in advance, then re-warm and assemble your burritos when ready.

YIELD: 8 burritos

stacked squash enchiladas

Stacked enchiladas make a perfect weeknight meal—simply assemble in a pie plate, bake, and serve. This version gets its lovely flavor from roasted yellow longneck and zucchini squashes, and is a wonderful way to make peace with veggie-resistant friends, family, and little ones. The question I most often get about stacked enchiladas is how to serve them. You can peel off and plate a layer at a time, but I actually opt to cut mine just like a layer cake into large wedges. Don't be surprised when even those veggie haters come back for a second slice of these enchiladas.

....

Preheat oven to 350°F.

Place the zucchini and yellow squash pieces along with the Hatch chile halves on a large rimmed baking sheet, toss with olive oil and a pinch of salt, and roast for 60 minutes. Remove from oven and set aside to cool slightly.

Place green onion pieces, lemon juice, and cooled squash and chile pieces in the bowl of a food processor fitted with a steel blade and process together to a uniform mixture. Season with cumin, coriander, and salt to taste, and pulse-process just to blend. Pour mixture into a large bowl.

Set up a small assembly line with your bowl of enchilada sauce, tortillas, cheese, and a 9-inch nonstick pie plate. Begin assembly by dipping each side of one tortilla in the sauce, then placing in the bottom of the pie plate. Note that this sauce is quite thick so don't worry if the sauce doesn't really adhere to the tortilla—you're just trying to dampen the tortilla. Next, spread a generous layer of the sauce on top of the tortilla and top with a sprinkle of

3 large zucchini, ends removed, cut into large chunks

2 large yellow longneck squash, ends removed, cut into large chunks

2 Hatch green chiles, stemmed, halved vertically (Anaheim chiles may be substituted)

1 tablespoon extra virgin olive oil

salt for roasting and seasoning to taste

8 green onions, ends removed, halved horizontally

juice of 1 large lemon

2 teaspoons ground cumin

1½ teaspoons ground coriander

6 7-inch corn tortillas

2 cups shredded Monterey Jack cheese

cheese. Repeat with the remaining tortillas. Once your stack is assembled top with any remaining cheese. Bake for approximately 20 minutes or until cheese is melted and tortillas are slightly crisp at the edges. You may opt to broil your enchiladas for an additional 1 to 2 minutes, just to crisp up the melted cheese on top. Remove baked enchiladas from oven, slice, and serve immediately.

YIELD: approximately 4 servings

fried avocado quesadillas with sweetest pico de gallo

For the Sweetest Pico de Gallo:

1 cup quartered seedless green grapes

1 cup quartered grape tomatoes

½ cup diced sweet onion

1 large jalapeño, minced (You may remove the seeds if you prefer to reduce the heat.)

2 stems parsley, minced

2 tablespoons freshly squeezed orange juice

For the quesadillas:

6 large avocados, peeled and pitted

¼ cup freshly squeezed lime juice

⅔ cup plain dry breadcrumbs (not panko)

2 teaspoons salt

2 teaspoons ground white pepper

2 tablespoons canola oil, divided

4 (9- or 10-inch) flour tortillas

2 cups shredded Chihuahua cheese (mild cheddar may be substituted)

Both the avocados and the quesadillas themselves receive a light pan-frying treatment in this lovely, surprisingly sweet dish. Crisping the avocado in advance affords a unique texture to each bite, especially when combined with a fruity grape and tomato version of *pico de gallo* salsa. Finish with creamy, melted cheese and you've got a hearty take on the quesadilla that will satisfy sweet and savory lovers alike.

To prepare the salsa, toss all of the ingredients together in a large bowl. Set aside.

To prepare the quesadilla filling, place the avocado flesh in a large bowl and mash to a chunky consistency. (Over-mashing the avocados here will make the work of frying much more difficult. I recommend retaining some of the chunks of the fruit's flesh in the finished mash.) Mix in the lime juice, breadcrumbs, salt, and pepper, stirring until evenly distributed. Heat 1 tablespoon of the canola oil in a 10-inch heavy-bottomed skillet, preferably cast iron, over medium heat. Once the oil is heated, add approximately half of the avocado mixture to the pan and spread loosely over its bottom. Cook for 2 to 3 minutes, until the underside of the avocado is crisped and golden brown. Flip the avocado and cook for another 2 to 3 minutes. (You want to cook this mixture as you would a hash, allowing even contact with the pan to ensure maximum crisping, and tossing with a spatula as carefully as possible.) Remove fried avocado to a paper-towel-lined baking sheet to drain slightly. Repeat with the remaining mixture.

To assemble and cook your quesadillas, remove the skillet from heat and line with a tortilla. Top with even layers of half of the fried avocado, half of the pico de gallo, and half of the cheese, finishing with a second tortilla. Using a sharp knife, carefully slice the quesadilla through into quarters. Return the skillet to the stove and cook over medium heat, applying slight pressure to the top of the quesadilla as it cooks. Fry until the edges are crisp and golden, approximately 3 to 4 minutes. Flip each quarter and cook for approximately 4 minutes more. Remove cooked quesadilla wedges and repeat with remaining ingredients. Serve immediately.

YIELD: 2 large quesadillas, 8 wedges

chipotle-spiced grilled cheese sandwiches

For the sandwiches:

7 plum (Roma) tomatoes, ends removed, sliced approximately ½-inch thick horizontally

extra virgin olive oil

½ cup unsalted butter, softened

2 tablespoons honey

8 thick slices crusted white bread

8 ounces Chihuahua cheese, sliced (medium or mild cheddar may be substituted)

For the Whole Grain Chipotle Mustard:

2 cups yellow mustard seeds

1 tablespoon coriander seeds

¾ cup plus 2 tablespoons white wine vinegar, divided

1 teaspoon granulated white sugar

1½ teaspoons salt

1½ tablespoons ground chipotle chile

1 teaspoon ground cumin

I believe that there are three keys to a perfectly executed grilled cheese sandwich: the melting of the cheese, the frying of the bread, and the flavor and textures of any extras that may find their way into the mix. This grilled cheese is my family's favorite—tart oven-roasted tomatoes, spicy whole grain mustard, sweet honey-infused butter, and of course, creamy melted cheese. Fried to crisp perfection, you might not be able to stop at just one.

Plum (Roma) tomatoes are perfect for roasting due to their meatier, less juicy makeup and high sugar content. I have found that roasting slowly at a lower temperature yields the best results, as does keeping your slices as uniform as possible when it comes to thickness.

To prepare the mustard, soak the mustard seeds and coriander seeds in ¾ cup water and ¾ cup of vinegar in a large bowl, covered and at room temperature, for 2 days. Once the soaking time has elapsed, place the mixture in the bowl of a food processor fitted with a steel blade and process with remaining ingredients until the desired consistency has been achieved. (Note that the seeds will not be completely pulverized and are not designed to be. The ideal finished product is the consistency of a chunky paste, perfect for spreading on sandwiches, tacos, etc. You'll likely want to keep your processing time to between 2 to 4 minutes, stopping to scrape down the sides of the bowl as necessary.) Store finished mustard in covered containers, preferably glass, for up to 3 months. This recipe yields approximately 2½ cups of mustard, more than enough for these sandwiches.

Preheat the oven to 350°F. Place tomato slices in an even layer on a parchment-lined baking sheet and drizzle

lightly with oil. Roast for approximately 75 minutes or until tomato pieces are shrunken, dried, and just starting to char at the edges. Remove to a large heat-proof bowl to cool.

In a small bowl, mix the softened butter and honey to a uniform paste and set aside.

Begin assembling your sandwiches by spreading a generous amount of the mustard on 4 pieces of bread and topping with the cheese slices, which should be evenly divided among the four sandwiches.

Mash the roasted tomatoes lightly with a fork and spread on top of the 4 remaining pieces of bread, again dividing evenly between all four. Put each of the sandwich halves together and top each with a generous spread of honey butter.

Heat a large skillet over medium-high heat and add one or two sandwiches to the heated pan, buttered-side down (depending on the size of your skillet and the size of your bread, you'll likely want to work in batches of no more than 2 sandwiches at a time). While the one side fries, butter the side facing up, and after approximately 2 minutes, carefully flip the sandwiches. Once you have cooked sides facing up, use your spatula to slightly compress the sandwiches, frying for just 2 more minutes. Finished sandwiches will be crisp and golden brown on the outside with the cheese melting on the inside. Remove from pan and serve immediately. Continue cooking the remaining sandwiches.

YIELD: 4 sandwiches

vegan puffy tacos with cumin-spiced hummus

For the taco shells (see sidebar on page 158):

4 cups canola oil for frying

6 small or medium vegan flour tortillas

For the Cumin-Spiced Hummus:

¼ cup sesame seeds

1½ cups cooked garbanzo beans

1½ teaspoons ground cumin

¾ teaspoon salt

½ teaspoon ground oregano (preferably Mexican oregano)

½ teaspoon ground white pepper

¼ cup extra virgin olive oil

¼ cup freshly squeezed lemon juice

For the taco filling:

1 pound parsnips, peeled, cut into 1- to 2-inch pieces

1 pound carrots, peeled, cut into 1- to 2-inch pieces

2 large turnips, ends removed, cut into 1- to 2-inch pieces

2 tablespoons extra virgin olive oil

1 teaspoon salt

1 teaspoon freshly ground black pepper

1 teaspoon ground ancho chile

Puffy tacos have become an iconic part of modern Southwestern cuisine. And is anyone really surprised? After all, puffy tacos are the marriage of a crisp, deep fried tortilla and the most achingly delicious filling that you can imagine. This vegan version involves perfectly puffy shells stuffed with slow-roasted root vegetables and a cumin-spiced hummus spread. These tacos have the texture, these tacos have the taste, these tacos have the will and the way to puff themselves right into your heart.

· ·

Note: The hummus spread and taco shells may be prepared well in advance of completing the filling and assembling the tacos. In fact, the hummus spread will keep, covered and refrigerated, for up to a week, and the taco shells will keep, sealed in a large container or zip-top bag, for up to two days. If serving these tacos to a crowd, I strongly recommend preparing your spread and shells in advance, thus enabling you to assemble and serve your puffy tacos when the filling is hot from the oven.

To prepare the taco shells, heat the canola oil in a large, heavy-bottomed pot until it registers 350°F on a candy or frying thermometer. Prick the tortillas through with a fork 4 to 6 times. Carefully add a tortilla to the oil and fry for 20 seconds on one side. The tortilla will sizzle vigorously on contact with the oil and will likely bubble on its surface. While it's frying you should only pierce large bubbles that inflate more than half of the tortilla, leaving any other smaller bubbles on the surface of the tortilla alone. After approximately 20 seconds the tortilla should have stopped sizzling and should boast a deep golden color on the side that has been fried. Flip and fry for 20 more seconds. Using your tongs, carefully fold the tortilla in half and hold it under the oil to cook for just 10 more seconds. Carefully remove the tortilla from the oil to a

paper-towel-lined baking sheet to drain, cool, and fully set its shape. It is important to carefully invert the folded cooked tortilla over the pot as you are removing it in order to drain off any hot oil that may be trapped inside the shell. The fried tortilla may still be flexible when you remove it from the oil but it will harden as it cools. Repeat with remaining tortillas.

To prepare the hummus, place the sesame seeds in a small, dry skillet over medium heat and toast, tossing often, for 4 to 5 minutes or until golden and fragrant. Remove to a spice grinder and pulverize to a paste. Place the sesame paste, garbanzo beans, cumin, salt, oregano, and white pepper into the bowl of a food processor fitted with a steel blade and process to a paste. With the food processor still running, stream the olive oil and lemon juice in through the feed tube and continue to process to a thick, uniform spread. Stop to scrape down the sides of the bowl as necessary. Set aside finished spread.

To prepare the taco filling, preheat the oven to 400°F. Toss the parsnip, carrot, and turnip pieces in a large bowl with the oil, salt, pepper, and ancho chile until all are well-coated. Spread in an even layer on a baking sheet and roast for 30 minutes. Remove from oven, toss, and return to the oven, roasting for 20 more minutes or until vegetables are fork tender. Set aside to cool. Once cool to the touch, coarsely chop all of the roasted vegetables together into slightly smaller pieces.

To assemble your tacos, spread the bottoms of each taco shell generously with a thick layer of the hummus and carefully top with the filling (you may need to crack the shells slightly to give yourself more room to add ample spread and filling). I recommend finishing these tacos with a tart salsa, such as the Salsa Verde on page 44. Serve immediately.

YIELD: 6 tacos

perfect puffy tacos: There are several keys to making perfect puffy tacos, starting with tortilla selection. I much prefer using flour tortillas over corn to make puffy taco shells. The reason? They puff more! It's just that simple. I also strongly recommend using smaller tortillas. Deep frying is not an easy job, and larger tortillas can be extremely difficult to manage when working over a pot of hot oil. If you are using store-bought tortillas, go with small (soft taco-size) 5- to 6-inch tortillas or medium (fajita-size) 7- to 8-inch tortillas. I also recommend piercing your tortillas through in several places with a fork. Pricking your tortillas prevents them from puffing up into an air-filled balloon during frying. The tortillas will still puff and bubble, so it's a good idea to keep that fork on hand during frying in case you need to deflate any oversized bubbles, but what you want to avoid is a single, huge tortilla balloon. Finally, frying tortillas is quick work so it's incredibly important to have all of your tools on hand and a production line set up. Use a frying thermometer to gauge the temperature of your oil at all times, and make sure to have a sturdy pair of metal tongs within reach. Your reward is warm, crispy, puffy taco heaven.

chicken tinga potpie

For the crust:

1½ cups all-purpose flour

1 teaspoon salt

¾ cup unsalted butter, chilled and cubed

3 tablespoons cold water

1 large egg, lightly beaten

For the filling:

2 pounds boneless, skinless chicken breasts

2 cups chicken stock

2 bay leaves

3 tablespoons extra virgin olive oil

1½ cups diced yellow onion

1 cup diced green bell pepper

2 cups chopped tomatillos

3 cups chopped plum (Roma) tomatoes

2 teaspoons minced fresh garlic

2 teaspoons fresh thyme

2 teaspoons fresh marjoram

1½ teaspoons salt, plus more for seasoning to taste if necessary

1½ teaspoons black pepper, plus more for seasoning to taste if necessary

Chicken Tinga is a fresh, flavorful poultry dish that, in my mind, is perfectly suited to serve as the filling in a luscious savory potpie. Think tender, saucy chicken paired with herbs, spices, and chunky vegetables, then tucked inside a rich, flaky butter crust. Even better, the filling and the pie crust dough can both be prepared in advance, then quickly assembled and baked for a hungry weeknight crowd.

To prepare the crust, place the flour and salt in the bowl of a food processor fitted with a steel blade and pulse-process just to blend. Add the butter and process to a coarse meal. With the motor still running, add the water through the feed tube and continue to process just until the dough comes together into a solid mass. Remove dough, form into a large disk, and set aside to rest. If preparing the dough in advance, wrap tightly in wax or parchment paper and store in the refrigerator for up to one day. Be sure to allow the dough to come to room temperature and soften slightly before rolling out.

To prepare the chicken, place chicken, stock, bay leaves, and 2 cups water in a large heavy-bottomed stockpot or Dutch oven and bring to a boil (be sure to select a vessel that allows the liquid to cover the chicken completely). Reduce to a simmer and cook for approximately 20 minutes or until the chicken is cooked through and fork-tender. Drain and cube the chicken into 2-inch pieces once cool enough to handle.

continued on next page

To prepare the sauce, heat olive oil in a large, heavy-bottomed pan over medium heat, add onions and bell pepper and sauté for 10 minutes. Add tomatillo and tomato pieces and cook for an additional 10 minutes. Lower heat to a simmer. Add the garlic, thyme, marjoram, salt, and black pepper and simmer for 10 final minutes. Stir cooked chicken pieces into the sauce and pour into a 9x13-inch baking pan.

Once you are ready to bake your potpie, preheat the oven to 400°F. Use a well-floured rolling pin to roll the dough out into an oblong shape with a thickness of approximately ¼ inch. I recommend rolling the dough out on a piece of parchment paper which you can then invert and carefully drape over the top of your filled baking pan, peeling away and discarding the paper once the dough is in place. Don't worry if your dough hangs over the edges of your pan in spots. Brush the surface of the dough with the beaten egg and lightly prick it several times with a fork to allow steam to vent.

Place your assembled pie onto a baking sheet and bake for approximately 45 minutes, or until the crust is golden brown at the edges and the filling is bubbling. Remove and serve immediately.

YIELD: approximately 4 servings

fancified frito pie

For the crust:

6 cups corn chips

¾ cup all-purpose flour

4 tablespoons unsalted butter, melted

2 large eggs, lightly beaten

For the chili:

2 pounds ground beef

1 28-ounce can crushed tomatoes in their juices

1 tablespoon ground cumin

1 tablespoon onion powder

1 tablespoon garlic powder

1 tablespoon ground ancho chile

1½ teaspoons ground white pepper

1 teaspoon salt

3 tablespoons masa harina

1 15-ounce can pinto beans, drained

1½ cups grated sharp cheddar cheese, plus more for serving (optional)

sour cream for serving (optional)

pickled jalapeños for serving (optional)

chopped fresh tomatoes for serving (optional)

Ah, Frito Pie … so kitschy … so guilt-inducing … so completely and totally irresistible. Frito Pie represents classic Americana casserole art at its best: crunchy corn chips, hearty chili, and toppings a-go-go, each serving personalized to suit each person at the table; meals just don't get any better than that. I've reinvented traditional Lone Star Frito Pie here, pressing the crushed corn chips into a fluted tart form to create an elegant shell. Finish your 'pie' with some of the best chili around and a healthy dose of melted cheese, and no one will think twice about digging in to this comely casserole.

. . . .

Preheat oven to 350°F.

To prepare the crust, place the corn chips in the bowl of a food processor fitted with a steel blade and process to a damp coarse meal. Remove to a large bowl and stir in the flour, butter, and eggs. Press the corn chip mixture into the bottom and up the sides of a 10-inch nonstick fluted tart pan, working to create as even a crust as possible. Bake for 30 minutes. (Because you are not working with a traditional pastry dough here, there is no need to blind bake this crust.) Remove the baked crust from the oven and set aside to cool and set.

Meanwhile, to prepare the chili, brown the beef in a large Dutch oven over medium heat, breaking up large pieces with the back of a wooden spoon as it cooks. Once the beef is no longer pink, drain off any fats in pan, then add the tomatoes, cumin, onion powder, garlic powder, ancho chile, white pepper, and salt. Bring to a boil, reduce heat, cover and simmer for approximately 25 minutes. After 25 minutes, stir in the masa harina and beans, and continue to simmer, uncovered, for an additional 45 to 60 minutes. Finished chili will be thick, chunky, and fragrant.

special equipment: You'll need a 10-inch nonstick fluted tart pan with a removable bottom to form the crust for this pie.

Remove cooked chili from heat and carefully pour into the prepared shell. Top with grated cheese and bake for 10 to 15 minutes just to set the pie and melt the cheese.

Remove pie from oven and set aside to cool for 10 minutes before unmolding; alternatively, you can serve it immediately right out of the tart pan. Note that, especially if serving straight from the oven, pieces of this pie will likely not hold their shape after slicing. After all, classic Frito Pie was meant to be enjoyed as a (delicious) hot mess. Optional toppings may be offered on the side.

YIELD: 6 servings

navajo tacos

6 pieces Navajo Fry Bread (page 30)

For New Mexico Green Chile Stew:

6 tablespoons extra virgin olive oil, divided

2 pounds boneless pork loin, cut into 2-inch cubes

1 large yellow onion, diced

1 tablespoon minced fresh garlic

¼ cup masa harina

3 cups reduced sodium beef stock

1 tablespoon ground cumin

1 tablespoon ground coriander

1 teaspoon ground oregano (preferably Mexican oregano)

3 cups Hatch green chiles, roasted, peeled, stemmed, and seeded (Anaheim chiles may be substituted)

salt to taste

ground white pepper to taste

Navajo Tacos entail freshly fried Navajo fry bread piled high with the toppings of your choice. If that doesn't catch your attention, consider this version that tops warm fry bread with rich, chunky New Mexico Green Chile Stew. The bread is crispy, the stew is bursting with flavor, and the finished taco is far greater than the sum of its parts. Note that New Mexico Green Chile is often made as a simple sauce (such as the one used in the Christmas-Style Seasoned Beef Burrito recipe found on page 220). This version is much more of a hearty stew, with a thick consistency and a generous helping of browned pork.

To prepare stew, heat 3 tablespoons of the olive oil in a large, heavy-bottomed Dutch oven or stockpot over medium-high heat until it just starts to smoke. Working in batches so pork is in a single layer, add pork pieces to the pan, turning carefully until each side is browned, 8 to 10 minutes total. Remove browned pork to a large bowl and continue with the next batch until all the pork has been browned. Once you are finished browning the pork, reduce the heat to medium and add the onion pieces and cook until tender, caramelized, and extremely fragrant, stirring occasionally, approximately 10 minutes. Add the garlic and cook for an additional 2 minutes. Add the masa harina and remaining 3 tablespoons of olive oil, stirring together and cooking 2 more minutes. Stir in the stock, cumin, coriander, oregano, and green chiles, and pork pieces, and bring to a boil. Reduce heat, cover and simmer 40 to 50 minutes, or until pork is cooked through and tender and stew is thick and fragrant.

As stew is cooking, warm fry bread in a 200°F conventional oven or toaster. Season finished stew with salt and white pepper to taste. Ladle over warmed fry bread and serve immediately.

YIELD: 6 servings

carne adovada cemitas

Cemitas hail from the Mexican state of Pueblo and are named for the seeded, sweet roll on which they are typically constructed; carne adovada is a New Mexican specialty of pork cooked in a rich red chile sauce. As far as I'm concerned, we're looking at a match made in heaven. The saucy, shredded meat goes wonderfully with fresh avocado, creamy melted cheese, and herbaceous cilantro. Consider having a bib on standby when digging into these gloriously sloppy sandwiches.

....

Cemitas typically involve a pretty specific set of ingredients. They start with the sweet, sesame-seed studded cemita poblana roll, which is made from an egg-based dough, similar to a brioche dough. Next comes the meat, usually deep-fried beef or saucy stewed pork. Toppings include melted mild cheese, such as Oaxacan string cheese or panela, avocado, fresh slices of white onion, and papalo, a leafy herb with a taste resembling cilantro. My version hits all the notes of a proper cemita with the added benefit of a bit of Southwestern flair.

3 pounds pork shoulder

1 tablespoon dried whole oregano

4 sprigs fresh thyme

2 sticks canela (cinnamon sticks may be substituted)

3 ounces New Mexican red chile pods, divided

4 cups chicken stock

1 tablespoon extra virgin olive oil

1 large yellow onion, diced

1 tablespoon minced fresh garlic

¾ cup apple cider vinegar

½ cup honey

1 tablespoon cumin

2 teaspoons ground white pepper

salt to taste

8 large sturdy sesame-topped sandwich rolls (or cemita rolls if available)

butter for rolls

2 cups shredded Oaxaca cheese (mozzarella cheese may be substituted)

4 avocados, pitted, peeled, thinly sliced

1 large white onion, thinly sliced

½ cup chopped fresh cilantro

To prepare the pork, place the pork, oregano, thyme, canela sticks, 2 of the New Mexican chile pods, stock, and 2 cups of water in the bowl of a slow cooker. You'll want to arrange the pork so it is completely submerged in liquid. Cook the pork on high for 4 to 4½ hours, or until just cooked through and fork tender, flipping the meat once about halfway through. Remove pork and shred with two forks, reserving 2 cups of the cooking liquid.

continued on next page

Meanwhile, to prepare the remaining chiles, remove the stems and as many of the seeds as possible from the chile pods and place the chile pods in a large heavy-bottomed stockpot over medium heat, stirring often to allow even toasting. After approximately 2 to 4 minutes, once pods are darkened and fragrant, add enough water to cover the chile pods, bring to a boil and cook for approximately 15 to 20 minutes, until chiles are tender and pliable, stirring often to ensure chiles are sumberged and cooking evenly. Remove chiles from heat and drain, discarding the cooking liquid.

To prepare the sauce, heat the olive oil in another pot and then add the yellow onion and sauté for approximately 10 minutes until tender, fragrant, and translucent. Add the garlic and cook for 2 more minutes. Remove the cooked onion and garlic to the bowl of a food processor fitted with a steel blade. Add the boiled chile pods, vinegar, honey, cumin, and white pepper to the food processor and process to a thick paste.

Place the sauce, shredded pork, and 2 cups of reserved cooking liquid from the slow cooker in the stockpot and bring to a boil. Reduce to a simmer, and continue to cook for 20 minutes, stirring occasionally, to thicken and reduce the sauce. Finish by seasoning with salt to taste.

To assemble your sandwiches, slice, toast, and butter your rolls. Top each with a generous spread of the warm meat mixture, then immediately apply the cheese so that it melts. Finish with slices of avocado, white onion, and a sprinkling of cilantro. Serve immediately.

YIELD: 8 large sandwiches

picadillo meatloaf with habanero ketchup

For the meatloaf:

3 pounds 80/20 ground beef

1 cup (approximately one 5-ounce jar) green olives, halved

½ cup (approximately one 4-ounce jar) capers

1 cup shredded carrots

½ cup dry plain breadcrumbs

2 large eggs

2 teaspoons freshly ground black pepper

2 teaspoons garlic powder

2 teaspoons onion powder

1 teaspoon cinnamon

1 teaspoon salt

continued on next page

Picadillo, a traditional dish of seasoned ground beef resembling a meat-based hash, is often prepared in large batches and served on festive occasions. Here, I've packed my take on picadillo into a flavorful meatloaf preparation, topping things off with homemade habanero ketchup. This recipe yields two large loaves so it's perfect for serving up at your next special gathering, especially because both the meat and the ketchup can be prepared days in advance of baking. A note for smaller-size crowds: don't be intimidated by the yield here as this recipe can easily be halved and also heats up wonderfully as leftovers.

Preheat oven to 350°F.

To prepare meatloaf, place all of the ingredients for the meatloaf in a very large bowl, and using clean hands, combine into a uniform mixture, taking care not to overwork the meat. (I find that clean hands are the best tool for mixing this large volume of ingredients; you just want to be sure that you start with a bowl large enough to allow you to do your job.) Divide the mixture in half and carefully press into 2 ungreased 9x5x3-inch loaf pans. Bake for 60 minutes.

continued on next page

For the Habanero Ketchup:

3 large orange tomatoes, chopped (preferably orange heirloom tomatoes)

½ large yellow onion, chopped

1 orange bell pepper, stemmed and seeded

1 habanero chile, stemmed, seeded, membranes removed

4 cloves garlic

2 tablespoons red wine vinegar

2 teaspoons ground cumin

2 teaspoons salt

1 teaspoon ground coriander

Meanwhile, to prepare the habanero ketchup, place the tomatoes, onion, bell pepper, habanero chile, and garlic cloves in the bowl of a food processor fitted with a steel blade and process until smooth. (You may work in batches if necessary.) Remove the processed mixture to a large stockpot and stir in the vinegar, cumin, salt, and coriander. Bring to a boil, reduce to a simmer, and cook for 20 to 25 minutes to thicken. Once ketchup has cooked down, remove from heat. This recipe yields approximately 3 cups of ketchup.

After the meatloaves have baked for 60 minutes, remove from oven, top each with half of the ketchup and bake for 10 more minutes, carefully broiling for the last few minutes, if desired, to caramelize the ketchup topping. Finished meatloaves will be cooked through, with the ketchup reduced, and just starting to caramelize across the top of each loaf.

YIELD: approximately 12 to 14 servings

coffee-rubbed lamb chops with weeknight mole

Succulent pan-fried lamb chops make a wonderful weeknight meal. These lusciously marinated chops are seasoned with coffee and sugar and paired with a rich mole sauce that also respects your busy schedule—put the lamb chops in the marinade the night before and the whole meal takes just 20 minutes to prepare. But don't let the timeline fool you, there's lovely flavor in each and every rich bite of this delicious dinner for two.

....

For lamb chops:

¼ cup extra virgin olive oil (I recommend using a good quality fruity olive oil here, such as a California olive oil.)

1 tablespoon instant espresso

½ teaspoon ground canela (cinnamon may be substituted)

½ teaspoon ground ancho chile

4 lamb loin chops, trimmed to a thickness of approximately 1 inch

To marinate the lamb chops, in a large ziptop bag toss the olive oil with the instant espresso, canela, and ancho chile. Add the lamb chops to the bag, seal, and toss well to coat. Marinate in the refrigerator until ready to cook; I recommend marinating these chops overnight for a really deep finished flavor.

To prepare the mole sauce, heat the olive oil in a large, heavy-bottomed sauté pan over medium heat. Add the onions and sauté until tender, fragrant, and translucent, approximately 10 minutes. Stir in the sugar, cocoa powder, peanut butter, raisins, and chicken broth and bring to a boil. Reduce to a simmer and cook for 5 more minutes.

For Weeknight Mole:

1 tablespoon extra virgin olive oil

½ cup diced yellow onion

2 teaspoons granulated white sugar

2 tablespoons unsweetened cocoa powder

2 tablespoons smooth peanut butter

¼ cup raisins

1½ cups chicken broth

To prepare the lamb chops, I recommend removing them from the refrigerator and allowing to come to room temperature before cooking. Once ready, heat a large, heavy-bottomed skillet over high heat. Add the lamb chops to the hot pan all at once along with any additional marinade that remains in the bag. Cook for just 3½ minutes per side for medium rare. Remove cooked chops and serve after resting for 5 minutes, topped with mole sauce.

YIELD: 2 servings

shredded chicken tacos with zuni succotash

8 soft corn tortillas, warmed

For the chicken:

2 pounds skinless boneless chicken breasts

2 cups low-sodium chicken stock

1 stick canela (cinnamon stick may be substituted)

2 serrano chiles, stemmed, halved vertically

2 bay leaves

1 28-ounce can crushed tomatoes in puree

4 chipotle chiles in adobo sauce, diced

1 tablespoon adobo sauce

For the Zuni Succotash:

1 tablespoon extra virgin olive oil

½ cup sunflower seeds

½ large yellow onion, diced

2 jalapeños, stemmed, minced

1 red bell pepper, stemmed, seeded, and diced

1¾ cups cooked pinto beans

1¾ cups cooked whole kernel corn

1 cup diced zucchini

1 cup low-sodium chicken stock

salt and freshly ground black pepper to taste

Shredded saucy chicken is practically made for stuffing into soft tacos. This version has the added benefit of being relatively low maintenance—you can cook the chicken in your slow cooker. Once you've shredded your meat, simply marry it with a rich tomato-based sauce, top it with a traditional Zuni crunchy vegetable succotash, and wrap everything up in soft, warmed corn tortillas. Dinner is served!

To prepare the chicken, place chicken breasts in the bowl of a slow cooker along with stock, canela stick, serrano chile pieces, and bay leaves. Cover and cook on high for approximately 4 to 4½ hours, or until chicken is just cooked through and fork tender. Remove chicken and shred with two forks, discarding remaining contents of slow cooker. Place shredded chicken in a large, heavy-bottomed Dutch oven along with tomatoes, diced chiles, and adobo sauce. Bring to a boil and then reduce to a simmer and cook for 30 minutes.

Meanwhile, to prepare the succotash, heat oil in a large, heavy-bottomed sauté pan over medium heat. Add the sunflower seeds, yellow onion, jalapeños, and red bell pepper, and cook for about 8 minutes. Stir in the pinto beans, corn, and zucchini, and cook for 5 more minutes. Add the stock, season to taste with salt and pepper, and bring to a boil. Reduce to a simmer, cover, and cook until vegetables are tender and liquid has been fully absorbed, approximately 15 to 17 minutes.

To assemble your tacos, top warmed corn tortillas generously with chicken and sauce, and finish with succotash. Serve immediately.

YIELD: 8 servings

from the grill

There's something about the taste of freshly grilled food that pairs perfectly with the flavors of the Southwest. And thanks to evolving grilling technique and new tools, there's virtually nothing that can't be cooked over hot coals or on a gas grill.

The recipes included in this chapter can be made on either type of grill and don't require any specialized tools beyond sturdy metal tongs and a spatula, as well as a basic grill basket for the herbaceous red snapper.

These recipes are also designed to be easily scaled up, since I know from personal experience that there's no fiesta like one that is planned around a hot grill. Some of my favorite memories are times spent with friends and family cooking out, which is why, from green-chile topped burgers to spiced up hot wings and a festive grilled apple pie, some of these dishes may feel a bit like party food. The fiesta is optional, however, so feel free to scale down or cook each recipe as is.

adobo chicken wings

4 pounds whole chicken wings,
    wing tips removed and
    discarded

salt

garlic powder

freshly ground black pepper

For the adobo sauce:

2 ancho chiles, stemmed and
    seeded

3 chipotle chiles, stemmed and
    seeded

4 cloves garlic

1 29-ounce can tomato puree

Note: These wings are an easy
make-ahead meal. Simply grill
the wings, toss in the prepared
sauce, spread onto parchment-
lined rimmed baking sheets
and keep warm in an oven set to
250°F for up to 1 hour.

I can't resist grilled chicken wings. I can't resist serving them up to a sports-watching, team-cheering crowd, and I can't resist feasting on them myself—and these wings never disappoint. Because chicken wings are already encased in a cap of fat that does such a good job of absorbing the smoky flavor of the grill, I like to start with completely dried wings coated in minimal seasoning. Once they are cooked, you'll toss them in a spicy adobo sauce that is the very definition of finger-licking good. Best get out your bib!

To prepare the adobo sauce, toast the chiles over a medium flame in a large, heavy-bottomed stockpot, stirring often, until just beginning to darken in color and become fragrant, approximately 2 minutes. Add 2 cups water, bring to a boil and cook until tender, approximately 15 to 20 minutes. Place the garlic in the bowl of a food processor fitted with a steel blade and process to a paste. Carefully pour the chiles and their cooking liquid into the food processor and process to a uniform liquid. Return the processed liquid to the stockpot, add the tomato puree and bring to a boil, reduce to low heat, and season with salt and black pepper to taste. Cook on low heat for approximately 60 minutes until sauce has thickened and flavors have married.

Preheat your grill to medium heat.

To prepare the wings, dry them thoroughly and season liberally with salt, garlic powder, and black pepper. Cook wings on covered preheated grill, skin side up, until the chicken is well-browned and not pink, approximately 25 to 30 minutes. Flip and cook skin side down, uncovered, for 5 more minutes or until skin is browned and crisp. Remove from grill, toss in adobo sauce, and serve.

YIELD: approximately 6 to 8 servings

chile-rubbed pork chops

Pork chops respond incredibly well to both dry rubs and grilling, which is why these smoky, spice-riddled, thick-cut chops are particularly winning. Even better, rubbed pork chops such as these are a snap to prepare and fantastic for serving to guests or even batching up and offering to a hungry crowd. Note that it is especially critical to allow these chops to rest after grilling—trust me, the result is worth the wait.

· ·

2 teaspoons garlic powder

2 teaspoons onion powder

2 teaspoons smoked paprika

2 teaspoons ground New Mexico red chiles

1½ teaspoons salt

1 teaspoon ground white pepper

1 teaspoon firmly packed light brown sugar

4 bone-in, thick-cut pork chops (approximately 1 inch thick)

To prepare the rub, toss together the garlic powder, onion powder, paprika, ground chiles, salt, white pepper, and brown sugar in a small bowl until well-combined.

Firmly and generously apply the rub to each side of the chops. Refrigerate until ready to grill, noting that the chops should be removed from refrigerator and allowed to return to room temperature before grilling.

Preheat your grill to medium heat.

Once you are ready to prepare the meat, place the chops on the grill at the spot where the grates are hottest, over direct flame if possible, and sear for 2 to 3 minutes per side. Move the seared chops to the indirect heat area of your grill, cover, and cook for 15 to 20 minutes or until the meat is cooked through. Remove from heat and set aside to rest for 5 minutes. Serve immediately after resting.

These chops pair wonderfully with a flavorful rice such as the Arroz Verde on page 141 or a sweet corn dish such as the Skillet-Baked Corn Pudding on page 130.

YIELD: 4 large pork chops

street-style corn

6 ears fresh corn, husks intact

4 chiles de árbol, stemmed and seeded

¼ cup peanuts

⅔ cup mayonnaise

salt to taste

freshly ground black pepper to taste

1 cup crumbled cotija cheese

chopped cilantro for garnish (optional)

lime juice for garnish (optional)

Whole kernel Mexican street-style corn on the cob, also known as *elote*, is a classic *antojito* (street food) that has thankfully found its way stateside. There are infinite ways to style your *elote*, topping it with any variety of spice, citrus, cream sauce, and/or cheese. Note that you'll want to grill the cobs with their husks still on in order to preserve the luscious juiciness of the fresh kernels. One thing is for sure, grilling takes this delicious dish to a whole new level.

Preheat your grill to high heat.

To prepare the ears, carefully peel back the husks of each without removing and strip away the silk. Return the husks to their place over the cleaned corn and set the ears aside.

To prepare the sauce, place the chiles in a dry pan or on a comal and toast over medium heat until darkened and fragrant, approximately 1 to 2 minutes. Remove to a spice grinder, process to a powder, and place in a medium bowl. Place the peanuts in the spice grinder and process to a coarse meal. (Take care not to overprocess the peanuts to a paste.) Remove the peanut meal to the same bowl as the ground chiles. Stir in the mayonnaise and season with salt and black pepper to taste. Set aside.

Cook corn on preheated grill, turning occasionally, until husks are charred on all sides, approximately 15 to 20 minutes. Remove grilled corn and set aside to cool for about 5 minutes before proceeding.

Spread the crumbled cheese out on a work surface. Carefully peel back the husks, and either tie off or remove the husks and fit each ear with a wooden

Note: Once you have grilled and dressed your corn, you may opt to serve it either by inserting a firm wooden stick in the base of each ear, or by simply leaving the peeled back husks in place and using them as a handle. For the stick route you will want to have sharpened wooden skewers on hand, and for the husk route you will want to have kitchen twine on hand to tie the leaves together.

skewer inserted into its base. (You may wish to use an oven mitt or kitchen towel to hold the hot corn as you work.) Generously coat each ear with the sauce, roll in the crumbled cheese, and top with chopped cilantro. Serve immediately, preferably with fresh lime wedges for garnish.

YIELD: 6 ears of corn

hatch chile cheeseburgers

20 ounces 80/20 ground beef

4 ounces lean ground pork

Salt and freshly ground black pepper

4 Hatch green chiles

4 thick-cut slices extra sharp cheddar cheese

4 sliced hamburger buns*

For the hamburger sauce:

2½ cups mayonnaise

¾ cup ketchup

½ cup dill pickle relish

1 tablespoon white distilled vinegar

1 tablespoon onion powder

1 teaspoon white granulated sugar

½ teaspoon salt

2 tablespoons minced fresh garlic

*I actually like to use telera-style sandwich buns here, as they are less bulky than conventional hamburger buns. Telera bread is occasionally sold in more ovoid shapes, so you'll want to be sure to select buns that are as circular as possible. In the absence of telera bread, any hamburger bun may be substituted.

Cheeseburgers like these can move mountains. Cheeseburgers like these can leap tall buildings in a single bound. Cheeseburgers like these could probably negotiate world peace, all while rescuing a herd of kittens from a tall tree. I kid you not when I tell you that these cheeseburgers are not only my family's absolute favorite, they are the very best burgers that I have ever had. Whether it is the moist, tender burgers themselves, or the perfectly designed combination of toppings, I have a feeling that you will keep coming back to this recipe time and time again, just as I do.

To prepare the burgers, place the beef and pork in a large bowl and season liberally with salt and black pepper. Taking care not to over work the meat, carefully form it into 4 patties, each approximately 4 inches in diameter. Use your thumb to make an indentation in the top of each patty. Place the prepared patties on a sheet of parchment paper and set aside in the refrigerator to rest for about 30 minutes.

Meanwhile, to prepare the fresh chiles, remove the stems of each and char the exterior of each completely, either by roasting over an open flame or slicing in half, spreading skin-side up onto a rimmed baking sheet, and roasting under a broiler. Once charred, carefully remove to a plastic ziptop bag or a large bowl and cover tightly with plastic wrap. Set aside for 5 minutes to allow the skin on the chiles to loosen. After 5 minutes, remove the chiles, and using a sharp knife or even your fingers, peel or scrape away the blackened skins from each. Slice off the tops and bottoms of each chile and dice the remaining flesh. You may opt to scrape away the

continued on next page

membranes and seed columns from each chile if you prefer to reduce their heat. Set the prepared chile pieces aside.

To prepare the sauce, whisk together the mayonnaise, ketchup, relish, and vinegar in a large bowl until thoroughly blended. Whisk in the onion powder, sugar, salt, and minced garlic. Transfer to a glass, air-tight container and store in the refrigerate until ready to use. (This recipe will yield quite a bit more sauce than needed for these burgers; store the leftovers in the refrigerator for up to 2 weeks—it will only get better with age.)

Once you are ready to cook and assemble your burgers, preheat your grill to high heat. Place the burgers on the heated grill, indented side up, and cook until marked and slightly charred on the bottoms, approximately 4 to 5 minutes. Flip and cook for 3 to 5 more minutes, depending on your desired degree of doneness. I recommend placing your sliced buns, cut side down, onto your grilling surface to toast lightly, although this is optional.

Remove cooked burgers and toasted buns from grill. Immediately top each burger with a slice of cheese. Slather both sides of each bun generously with some sauce, place burger on each bun, top with a generous helping of the diced chiles, and serve immediately.

YIELD: 4 hamburgers and approximately 4½ cups of sauce

pomegranate & lime chicken thighs

For the thighs:

1 cup Greek yogurt

½ cup pomegranate juice

1 teaspoon salt

1 teaspoon garlic powder

4 bone-in, skin-on chicken thighs

Pomegranate arils for garnish
(optional)

**For the Pomegranate & Lime
Glaze:**

2 cups pomegranate juice

½ cup granulated white sugar

¼ cup freshly squeezed lime
juice

2 tablespoons honey

2 tablespoons Dijon mustard

Admittedly I didn't become a fan of chicken thighs until
later in life, but now that I've seen the light I'm constantly
looking for new ways to prepare them. I particularly like to
marinate the bone-in, skin-on version in a well-seasoned
yogurt blend, such as the bright, pomegranate-infused
version featured here. The meat stays moist on the bone
and a last minute flip renders the skin perfectly crisp. Top
everything off with a super sweet pomegranate and lime
glaze, and you'll have as many fans as the chicken thighs
you're serving.

To marinate chicken, combine the yogurt, pomegranate
juice, salt, and garlic powder in a ziptop bag. Add the
chicken thighs and toss well to coat. Refrigerate for at
least 2 hours or up to overnight.

Once you are ready to cook the thighs, preheat your grill
to medium heat.

To prepare the glaze, place the pomegranate juice,
sugar, lime juice, honey, and mustard in a small
saucepan, whisk together and bring to a boil. Reduce to
a simmer and cook until thickened, approximately 20 to
25 minutes. Remove from heat and set aside.

Meanwhile, place thighs skin side up on heated grill,
cover, and cook until chicken has browned and is no
longer pink, approximately 25 to 30 minutes. Uncover,
flip thighs, and cook for just 2 to 3 minutes more to
crisp and slightly char the skins. Remove cooked thighs,
top with glaze, garnish with arils, if desired, and serve
immediately.

YIELD: 2 servings

citrus & herb red snapper

Red snapper is a lovely, flaky whitefish that is firm and flavorful enough to hold up wonderfully on the grill. It pairs perfectly with fresh herbs and citrus juices, which is what I have set up here. I recommend using an appropriately sized grilling basket to hold your fillets and herbs. If you cannot find red snapper at your local market, rockfish, catfish, monkfish, or any type of seabass are acceptable substitutes.

....

4 5-ounce to 6-ounce red snapper
 fillets

¼ cup extra virgin olive oil

¼ cup freshly squeezed lime
 juice

2 tablespoons chopped parsley

2 tablespoons chopped cilantro

1 tablespoon minced fresh garlic

1 bunch whole green onions,
 ends removed

Place the fish fillets in a shallow dish. Whisk the oil and lime juice together in a small bowl. Whisk in the parsley, cilantro, and garlic, and pour over the fillets, turning each to coat. Set aside to marinate for 30 minutes.

Meanwhile, preheat your grill to medium heat.

Place the marinated fillets along with the green onions in your grill basket and grill over medium indirect heat until the fish is cooked through and opaque and onions are slightly charred, approximately 4 to 6 minutes per side. Remove cooked fish and onions to a large serving platter and serve immediately.

YIELD: 4 servings

grilled apple pie

Grilled fruit makes for such a delicious dessert. And when it's piled high inside a tender, sweet pastry crust, there's not a much better way to finish a meal. Tart, sturdy apples stand up well to both the grill and the oven here, absorbing the smoky flavors of your barbecue and then the buttery richness of the pastry crust. Prepare yourself for messy goodness as there's nothing prim or proper about this gloriously sticky-sweet grilled fruit pie.

For the crust:

1½ cups all-purpose flour, plus more for dusting

2 tablespoons granulated white sugar

½ teaspoon salt

8 tablespoons unsalted butter, chilled and cubed

4 tablespoons cold water

For the filling:

½ cup light agave nectar

½ cup firmly packed light brown sugar

1 teaspoon ground canela (cinnamon can be substituted)

½ teaspoon salt

4 large, tart apples, such as Granny Smiths, peeled, cored and sliced into ½-inch thick rounds

¼ cup freshly squeezed lemon juice

¼ cup canola oil

Preheat the oven to 425°F and the grill to medium heat.

Line a 9-inch pie plate with parchment paper and set aside.

To prepare the crust, place the flour, sugar, and salt in the bowl of a food processor fitted with a steel blade and pulse-process just to combine. Add the cold pieces of butter and process to a coarse meal. With the motor running, add the cold water through the feed tube and process just until a solid mass of dough forms. Remove the dough, divide in two, and wrap each piece tightly in wax or parchment paper. Refrigerate for 1 hour.

Meanwhile, to prepare the filling, stir the agave nectar, brown sugar, canela, and salt together in a large bowl and set aside. Toss the apple slices with the lemon juice and oil in a separate bowl. Grill the apple slices until just tender and lightly marked, turning once, approximately 6 minutes total. Remove grilled apple slices to the large bowl with the brown sugar mixture and immediately toss well to coat. Set aside to macerate and cool slightly.

Once the dough has chilled through, use a well-floured rolling pin to roll out one piece of the dough on a well-floured surface to a thickness of approximately ¼ inch.

Carefully drape the rolled dough over the prepared pie plate, pressing it gently into place and trimming the edges to fit the rim of the plate. Layer the apple slices in the crust until all are used. Pour any remaining brown sugar mixture in the bowl over the stacked apples. Roll out the second piece of dough the same way and drape over the apples. Trim excess and pinch top and bottom crust edges together, crimping as desired. Slash crust in center to vent.

Bake for 30 minutes or until the edges are deep golden brown and the filling is bubbling. Remove from heat and set aside to cool slightly before serving. This pie is especially delicious when served warm with cajeta (page 38) generously ladled over top.

YIELD: approximately 8 servings

desserts

Your sweet tooth needs some love after all of those savory salsas, and man, do I have the ticket for you! While most people don't typically think 'sweet' when they think about Southwestern cuisine, there are actually a number of flavors that are common to this style of cooking. Think caramel, think anise, think sticky coconut, and, of course, think warm spicy canela.

As with the other recipes included in this book, you'll find that I like to play with my desserts just a bit. Which is why I've included my recipes for pear-flavored almond crusted tres leches cake, flaky empanada pastries stuffed with everyone's favorite combination of peanut butter and jelly, and classic sugar cookies punched up with some nutty browned butter.

Along with my trusty food processor, my stand mixer is my right-hand man when it comes to preparing desserts in my kitchen. Stand mixers make easy work out of the tedious tasks of whipping and creaming, so I count on mine often. That said, there's absolutely no reason why a hand-held mixer won't fit the bill when working on any of the proceeding recipes.

chia cupcakes

Chia plants were cultivated by the Aztec people in pre-Columbian times, which explains why chia seeds have long been a part of Mexican cuisine. Thankfully, chia seeds have recently become known stateside for more than their ability to adorn a stone pet as they are rich in omega-3 fatty acids and boast a deliciously appealing nutty flavor. Here, the seeds are spun into lovely cupcakes, the end result being a light crumb with a delightful crunch. Be sure to take a moment to toast your chia seeds before folding them into your batter to release their naturally delicious oils.

For the cupcakes:

1 cup chia seeds

2 cups all-purpose flour

2 teaspoons baking powder

½ teaspoon salt

½ cup vegetable oil

1 cup firmly packed dark brown sugar

2 large eggs

½ cup buttermilk

3 tablespoons honey

1 teaspoon vanilla extract

For the cream cheese frosting:

12 ounces whipped cream cheese

1 cup confectioners' sugar

½ cup whole milk

2 teaspoons ground canela (cinnamon may be substituted)

Preheat oven to 350°F.

Line the cups of two standard (12-cup) muffin tins with paper liners and set aside.

Place the chia seeds in a dry pan over medium heat and toast, tossing often, for 3 to 5 minutes, or until seeds become slightly darker in color and fragrant. Remove from heat and set aside to cool.

To prepare the cupcakes, whisk together the flour, baking powder, and salt in a large bowl. Set aside. In another large bowl, cream together the vegetable oil and brown sugar. Beat in the eggs, one at a time, followed by the buttermilk, honey, and vanilla extract. Slowly beat in the dry ingredients, mixing just until you have a uniform batter. Fold in the toasted chia seeds. Divide batter among prepared muffin cups (a 3 tablespoon scoop works well for this). Bake cupcakes for 22 to 24 minutes or until they are puffed, golden brown, and a cake tester inserted into the center of one comes out clean. Remove baked cupcakes from oven and set aside to cool before frosting.

To prepare the frosting, place cream cheese, confectioners' sugar, milk, and canela in the bowl of a stand mixer and mix on low speed just to blend. Once ingredients are combined, increase speed to high and whip frosting until light and fluffy, approximately 2 minutes. Top each cooled cupcake generously with frosting.

YIELD: 24 cupcakes

pistachio polverones

1 cup pistachio kernels

1 cup unsalted butter, softened

½ cup granulated white sugar

2 large egg yolks

1 teaspoon vanilla extract

2 cups all-purpose flour

⅔ cup confectioners' sugar

These sweet, shortbread-like cookies are extremely difficult to resist. They require no leavening and, as a result, are incredibly dense, rich, and buttery. Often known throughout the United States as Mexican wedding cookies and served south of the border at weddings and other special celebrations, this version is made even more festive with the incorporation of toasted pistachios.

Preheat oven to 350°F.

Spread the pistachio kernels in an even layer on a rimmed baking sheet and toast in the oven for 5 to 7 minutes or until fragrant and slightly golden. Remove from oven and set aside to cool.

Cream butter and granulated sugar together until light and fluffy. Beat in the egg yolks and vanilla. Add flour and mix just until you have a uniform, stiff dough.

Coarsely chop the cooled pistachios. Fold into the dough, using clean hands if necessary to gently work the pistachio pieces throughout. Place finished dough on a large sheet of parchment paper and shape into a log approximately 2 to 3 inches in diameter. Wrap tightly and refrigerate until firm, at least 2 hours.

Once the dough is chilled through and you are ready to bake your cookies, preheat the oven again to 350°F. Slice the dough log into ½-inch-thick slices and place on a parchment-lined baking sheet (these cookies will not spread so you can fit up to 16 on a standard-sized half sheet pan). Bake for approximately 25 to 28 minutes. Finished cookies will be firm and just turning light golden brown on the bottoms. (Note: if you bake your cookies straight from the refrigerator, you may need to leave them in the oven for up to 30 minutes. But that said, overbaking these cookies is not good, so start checking for doneness at 20 minutes.)

Remove baked cookies from oven and cool for 5 to 10 minutes on the cookie sheet. Place the confectioners' sugar in a small bowl and toss the still-warm cookies in the confectioners' sugar. The key is to toss the cookies in the sugar when they are not so hot that the sugar will melt, but warm enough that it will adhere to the exterior of the cookies. Place finished cookies on a rack to cool and set completely.

YIELD: approximately 25 cookies

dulce de leche layer cake with sweet pecan 'pesto'

For the cakes:

2½ cups all-purpose flour

2 teaspoons baking powder

1 teaspoon salt

1 cup vegetable oil

1 cup granulated white sugar

2 large eggs

1¼ cups dulce de leche

1 teaspoon vanilla extract

1 cup buttermilk

For the Sweet Pecan Pesto:

4 cups whole pecans

1 14-ounce can sweetened condensed milk

1 teaspoon ground ancho chile

2 teaspoons ground canela (cinnamon may be substituted)

½ cup whole milk

½ cup sour cream

Classic layer cakes are so comforting, so delicious, and so fun to serve at special occasions. This eye-popping take on tradition involves moist layers flavored with sweet dulce de leche caramel sauce, and frosted with a pecan 'pesto.' The nutty topping is sticky, crunchy, and a snap to prepare; it encases the sponge cakes and lends itself to being enjoyed right out of the mixing bowl. I recommend delighting your friends and family by serving this sweet, satisfying cake at your next fiesta.

Preheat oven to 350°F.

Line 2 circular 9-inch cake pans with parchment paper and set aside.

To prepare the cakes, whisk the flour, baking powder, and salt together in a large bowl. Set aside. In another large bowl, cream together the vegetable oil and sugar. Beat in the eggs, one at a time, followed by the dulce de leche and vanilla extract. Slowly beat in the dry ingredients, alternating with the buttermilk and mixing just until you have a uniform batter. Divide batter among prepared cake pans. Bake cakes for 32 to 35 minutes or until a cake tester inserted into the center of one comes out clean. Remove baked cakes from the oven and set aside to cool before unmolding.

Meanwhile, to prepare the pecan pesto, spread the pecans in an even layer on a rimmed baking sheet and bake for 5 to 7 minutes or until fragrant and slightly darkened in color. Remove and set aside to cool slightly. Once pecans are cool enough to handle, place in the bowl of a food processor fitted with a steel blade and add the condensed milk, ancho chile, canela, milk, and sour cream and process to a thick, uniform paste.

To assemble the cake, unmold layers and remove parchment paper. Place bottom layer, bottom side-down, on a large rimmed serving platter and top generously with a thick layer of the pecan pesto. Top with second layer, also bottom side-down, and finish by pouring remaining pecan pesto over top (a rimmed serving platter is recommended here, as this recipe yields quite a bit of pecan pesto and some of it will likely puddle at the sides of the cake). This cake will keep well for up to 3 days.

YIELD: approximately 12 to 14 servings

hello, dolly! bars

1 sleeve graham crackers (9 whole crackers)

1 disk (3.15 ounces) Mexican chocolate, chopped*

6 tablespoons unsalted butter, melted

1 teaspoon ground ancho chile

1 cup pecans

½ cup pumpkin seeds, hulled

1 cup shredded sweetened coconut

1 cup butterscotch chips

1 14-ounce can sweetened condensed milk

*Note: Especially if it has been sitting in your pantry for a while, Mexican chocolate can be quite hard. I strongly recommend taking a moment to chop it into smaller pieces before processing, just to reduce the workload of your food processor by a bit and ensure a more even finished product.

While the origin of the moniker for these bars is somewhat obscure, their appeal surely isn't. They are basically a kitchen sink of sweet flavors and textures, with something for just about everyone. This version involves a thick graham cracker crust speckled with Mexican chocolate and ground ancho chiles, topped off with crunchy pumpkin seeds and pecans, and finished with chewy coconut and butterscotch chips. Call them whatever you want, these super-satisfying dessert bars are one of my personal favorites.

Preheat oven to 350°F.

Line a 9-inch square baking pan with parchment paper and set aside.

Break graham crackers into large pieces and place in the bowl of a food processor fitted with a steel blade. Add the Mexican chocolate pieces, melted butter, and ancho chile. Process the ingredients until they are the consistency of wet sand. Press firmly into the bottom of your prepared pan.

Coarsely chop the pecans, pumpkin seeds, and coconut and place in a large bowl. Add the butterscotch chips and condensed milk, stirring all ingredients together to coat evenly. Spread mixture in an even layer over the crust. Bake for 40 to 45 minutes. Finished bars will be deep golden brown and crisp at the edges. Remove from oven and set aside to cool and set in the pan for at least 30 minutes before cutting and serving.

YIELD: 9 large bars

bizcochito ice cream sandwiches

For the Anise Ice Cream:

1½ tablespoons anise seeds

1½ cups heavy cream

¾ cup whole milk

½ cup granulated white sugar

½ teaspoon salt

3 large egg yolks

For the cookies:

2½ cups all-purpose flour, plus
    more for dusting

1½ teaspoons baking powder

½ teaspoon salt

1 teaspoon ground canela
    (cinnamon may be
    substituted)

1 cup vegetable shortening

¾ cup granulated white sugar

2 large eggs

1 teaspoon vanilla extract

1 tablespoon grated orange zest

special equipment: You will
need an ice cream machine with a
capacity of at least two-quarts to
prepare this ice cream.

What's more fun than an ice cream sandwich? An ice cream sandwich made with bizcochitos and anise ice cream, for sure! Think sweet little crisp wafer cookies held together with a healthy scoop of rich ice cream. The cookies are warmly flavored with cinnamon and vanilla, while the ice cream boasts the unique licorice-like flavor of toasted anise seed. And since bizcochitos are the official state cookie of New Mexico, it's not hard to believe that these ice cream sandwiches are destined to become the official dessert of choice in your *casa*.

To prepare the ice cream, place the anise seeds in a dry pan and toast over medium heat for 3 to 5 minutes or until they are fragrant and slightly darkened in color. Remove to a spice grinder and grind to a powder. Set aside to cool. Meanwhile, bring the heavy cream, milk, sugar, and salt to a boil in a large saucepan. Place the egg yolks in a large bowl and once the cream mixture is boiling, whisk half of it into the yolks. Adjust the heat under the remaining cream mixture down to low, whisk the yolk mixture back into the pan, and continue to cook on low heat until the mixture is thick enough to coat the back of a metal spoon, about 5 minutes. Remove the cream mixture from the heat and pour it through a fine mesh sieve into a covered container and place in the freezer to chill. Once your custard has chilled through, stir in the ground anise seeds, put the seasoned custard into your ice cream maker and freeze according to the manufacturer's instructions. Once fully churned, remove the ice cream from the maker and freeze overnight.

To prepare the cookies, sift the flour, baking powder, salt, and canela together in a large bowl, and set aside. In another large bowl, cream together the shortening and sugar until light and fluffy. Add the eggs one at a time, then the vanilla and the orange zest, beating until blended. Slowly add the dry ingredients, again beating just until blended. This dough is extremely stiff and you may need to knead in the last of the dry ingredients by hand. Once you have a solid, uniform dough, shape it into a large disk, wrap in parchment paper, and refrigerate for 1 hour.

Once dough has chilled through, preheat oven to 350°F.

Using a well-floured rolling pin, roll dough out on a well-floured work surface to a thickness of approximately ¼ inch. Cut out cookies using a 3-inch cutter and remove to parchment-lined baking sheets placing about 3 inches apart. Bake for 18 to 20 minutes or until cookies are slightly golden at their edges and on their bottoms. Remove cookies from baking sheet to a rack or sheet of parchment paper to cool.

To assemble your ice cream sandwiches, scoop some ice cream onto one cookie and top with another, applying pressure to create a solid sandwich. I recommend using a dull knife dipped in warm water to smooth the sides of your sandwiches and assembling them in advance of serving. Place them in the freezer just after assembling to set up and firm their shape.

You will likely have additional ice cream left over that you may simply cover and store in the freezer for later enjoyment.

YIELD: approximately 12 large ice cream sandwiches

peanut butter & jelly empanadas

For the crust:

1½ cups all-purpose flour, plus more for dusting

2 tablespoons granulated white sugar

½ teaspoon salt

12 tablespoons unsalted butter, chilled and cubed

3 tablespoons cold water

For the filling:

¾ cup crunchy peanut butter (or smooth if you prefer)

¾ cup prickly pear, strawberry, or raspberry preserves*

*Any flavor of preserves will work here, so use your favorite, but I do recommend going with a thicker jam or even a marmalade or chutney, and avoiding a thinner jelly.

Let's face it, peanut butter and jelly brings out the kid in all of us. Tuck that glorious combo into a delicate pastry crust and watch things quickly go from good to positively giddy. I love serving these sweet hand pies at large gatherings when people are milling around and portable desserts are at a premium (the recipe easily doubles to accommodate this). They also keep well and will score you tons of points when you pack one into someone special's lunchbox.

....

Preheat oven to 425°F.

Line two rimmed baking sheets with parchment paper and set aside.

To prepare the crust, place the flour, sugar, and salt in the bowl of a food processor fitted with a steel blade and pulse-process just to combine. Add the cold pieces of butter and process to a coarse meal. With the motor running, add the cold water through the feed tube and process just until a solid mass of dough forms. Remove the dough, wrap tightly in wax or parchment paper, and refrigerate for 1 hour.

Meanwhile, to prepare the filling, stir the peanut butter and preserves together in a large bowl; they don't need to be completely blended, just swirled together into a single solution.

continued on page 209

Once the dough has chilled through, use a well-floured rolling pin to roll it out on a well-floured surface to a thickness of approximately ¼ inch. Using a 4-inch round cookie cutter or even an inverted saucer with a diameter of approximately 4 inches as a guide, cut out 8 rounds, reforming and rerolling dough as needed.

Spoon 2 to 3 tablespoons of the filling directly onto the center of each round and fold in half, pinching the edges of each half-circle together to seal. Cut a small vent in the top of each empanada.

Place on the prepared baking sheets 3 inches apart, and bake for approximately 20 minutes. Finished empanadas will be golden brown across the top and at the edges. Remove and set aside to cool slightly before serving or storing.

YIELD: 8 large empanadas

almond-crusted pear tres leches cake

For the crust:

9 whole graham crackers

½ cup almonds

½ cup almond meal

8 tablespoons unsalted butter, melted

For the cake:

1½ cups all-purpose flour

1 tablespoon baking soda

4 large eggs

1½ cups granulated white sugar

½ cup whole buttermilk

For the soak:

¼ cup whole milk

1 (14 ounce) can sweetened condensed milk

1 (12 fluid ounce) can evaporated milk

½ cup pear juice

Tres leches (three milks) cakes are pretty much dessert perfection. What's not to love about a sweet sponge cake soaked in luscious cream sauce? This particular spin on a classic tres leches cake involves a toasted almond crust and a pear-flavored soak; the nutty crunch from the crust pairs wonderfully with the moist crumb of the soaked cake. It's rich, it's flavorful, and it's absolutely impossible to resist.

Preheat oven to 350°F.

Line a 9-inch springform cake pan with a depth of at least 3 inches with parchment paper and set aside.

To prepare the crust, break the graham crackers into large pieces and place with the whole almonds in the bowl of a food processer fitted with a steel blade. Process to a coarse meal. Remove to a large bowl and toss together with the almond meal and melted butter. Spread the very damp mixture over the bottom of the prepared pan and bake for 10 minutes. Remove and set aside to cool.

Meanwhile, to prepare the cake, whisk the flour and baking soda together in a large bowl, and set aside. In another large bowl, beat together the eggs and sugar. Slowly beat in the dry ingredients, alternating with the buttermilk and mixing just until you have a uniform batter. Pour the batter over the crust and bake for 45 to 50 minutes or until a cake tester inserted into the center of the cake comes out clean. Remove baked cake from oven and set aside to cool for at least 10 minutes before unmolding.

continued on next page

Meanwhile, to prepare the soak, whisk the whole milk, condensed milk, evaporated milk, and pear juice together in a large bowl. Once the cake has cooled, release it from the pan, remove the parchment paper, and set the cake on a rimmed platter. Using a wooden skewer, poke a series of holes through the top of the cake and pour the soak over top. Set the cake aside to allow the soak to be absorbed. The cake can be served chilled from the refrigerator or at room temperature.

YIELD: approximately 8 to 10 servings

brown butter coyotas

1 cup unsalted butter

2 cups firmly packed dark brown
    sugar

2 large eggs

½ teaspoon vanilla extract

2 cups all-purpose flour

1½ teaspoons baking soda

¾ teaspoon ground canela
    (cinnamon may be
    substituted)

½ teaspoon salt

Coyotas are traditional Mexican cookies that were surely designed to showcase the mapley-sweet flavor of dark brown sugar. So what could be better than introducing some nutty brown butter into the mix? Nothing, I tell you. Don't be deceived by the simplicity of these large, chewy cookies—their deep, layered flavors will keep you coming back for more.

Preheat oven to 350°F.

To brown the butter, place it in a large, heavy-bottomed pan over medium heat. (If possible, it is ideal to use a pan with a light-colored interior in order to best monitor the progress of the butter as it browns.) The butter will foam, turn yellow and eventually brown; be sure to stir it regularly in order to keep the milk solids, which may pop and crackle as the butter cooks, from settling to the bottom of the pan. Once the butter is a deep brown color and has a strong nutty aroma, immediately pour it into a large heatproof bowl to cool.

After the browned butter has cooled slightly, add the brown sugar and beat together for just a few minutes. Add the eggs and vanilla extract and continue to mix just until incorporated.

Whisk the flour, baking soda, canela, and salt together in a medium bowl. Add the dry ingredients to the butter mixture, mixing just until a uniform dough has formed (this dough is quite damp and dark, closely resembling wet sand).

Shape dough into large balls (a 3-tablespoon self-ejecting scoop works really well here) and arrange on

parchment-lined baking sheets. These cookies, just like traditional coyotas, are designed to spread quite a bit as they cook so don't put any more than six at a time on a standard large baking sheet.

Bake cookies for 14 to 16 minutes or until they are spread, cracked, and slightly puffed. Remove cookies from the baking sheet to a rack or sheet of parchment paper and set aside to cool.

YIELD: approximately 18 large cookies

feast day cookies

These diminutive cookies pack a flavorful punch like you won't believe. They derive their crumbly, crisp texture from vegetable shortening; their rich, buttery flavor from toasted pinyon nuts; and their sweet, aromatic taste from whole anise seeds. Simply roll out your dough, cut your cookies, bake, and watch the line form outside your kitchen. Warm from the oven, these traditional celebratory cookies will always draw a crowd.

....

1 teaspoon anise seed

½ cup pinyon nuts (pinenuts may be substituted)

¾ cup vegetable shortening

1¼ cups granulated white sugar, divided

2 large eggs

1 teaspoon vanilla extract

2 cups all-purpose flour

1 teaspoon baking powder

½ teaspoon salt

1 teaspoon ground canela (cinnamon may be substituted)

Preheat oven to 350°F.

To prepare the anise seeds, spread them in an even layer in a small, dry fry pan and toast over a medium flame for just 2 minutes, agitating several times while toasting. Set aside to cool.

To prepare the pinyon nuts, spread them in an even layer in a large, dry fry pan and toast over a medium flame for just 2 to 4 minutes, agitating several times while toasting. (I toast my pinyon/pinenuts on my stovetop as opposed to in the oven because they burn so quickly that I prefer being able to watch them closely; you'll want to keep an eye on yours and toss often as they brown.) Remove from heat when the nuts have turned light golden brown and are fragrant. Once cooled to the touch, coarsely chop and set aside.

To prepare the cookies, in a large bowl, beat together the shortening and ¾ cup sugar until light and fluffy. Add the eggs one at a time, then the vanilla, beating until blended.

Whisk the flour, baking powder, salt, and cooled anise seeds together in another bowl. Slowly add the dry ingredients to the shortening mixture, mixing just until you have a dry, crumbly, but uniform dough. Fold in the nut pieces.

Roll the dough out on a well-floured board using a well-floured rolling pin to a thickness of approximately ¼ inch. Cut out cookies using a 2½-inch round cutter and place on parchment-lined baking sheets (these cookies will not spread so you can fit up to 16 on a standard-sized half sheet pan). Before baking, whisk remaining ½ cup sugar and canela together in a small bowl and top unbaked cookies with a generous dusting of the mixture. Bake for just 14 to 16 minutes or until cookies are slightly browned at the edges and across their bottoms. Remove finished cookies from baking sheet to a rack or sheet of parchment paper to cool or enjoy warm from the oven.

YIELD: approximately 32 cookies

a christmas-style extra

To be honest, I'm one of those people who goes a little nutty bananas over the end of the year holiday season. I'll string lights up around the cacti in our front yard and prepare *fiestas* and themed meals for friends and family, and I've even been known to (attempt to) rock a Mrs. Claus costume. I just can't help myself. So it shouldn't come as any surprise that the classic New Mexican tradition of offering food served up 'Christmas-style' was one of my most beloved discoveries when it comes to Southwestern cuisine.

Chiles and the chili dishes that they season are serious business in New Mexico, so much so that, in the late 1990s, the New Mexico State Legislature declared 'Red or Green?' to be the official state question. Not to worry if you're a fence sitter or just happen to enjoy having your plate lit up with the colors of the nativity season: simply order your enchiladas, tacos, or in this case, succulent shredded beef burritos, served 'Christmas'; you'll receive your meal slathered in a hearty helping of both red and green chilis.

Best of all, this vibrant, equal-opportunity style of service isn't restricted to just one season. You'll find Christmas-style offerings available any time of the year in the Southwest, which means you can feel free to serve these satisfying burritos whenever you're feeling festive.

christmas-style seasoned beef burritos

For the beef:

2 cups beef stock

½ cup extra virgin olive oil

½ cup apple cider vinegar

2 tablespoons minced fresh garlic

1 teaspoon allspice berries

4 pounds beef chuck pot roast

4 serrano chiles, stemmed and
    halved vertically

1 large sweet yellow onion,
    coarsely chopped

For the green chili:

6 tablespoons extra virgin olive
    oil, divided

1 large yellow onion, diced

1 tablespoon minced fresh garlic

3 cups Hatch green chiles,
    roasted, peeled, stemmed,
    and seeded (Anaheim chiles
    may be substituted)

6 sprigs parsley

3 tablespoons all-purpose flour

1 tablespoon ground cumin

1 tablespoon ground coriander

1 teaspoon ground oregano
    (preferably Mexican oregano)

1 cup beef stock

salt to taste

ground white pepper to taste

To prepare the beef, whisk the stock, olive oil, vinegar, garlic, and allspice berries together in the bowl of a crockpot. Halve the roast into two large pieces and place into the liquid. Top with the serrano chiles and onion, cover and cook on high for 1 hour. Reduce heat to low and cook for 5 hours until the beef is cooked through and easily shredded. Remove beef from crockpot, discard cooking liquid and vegetables, and once the beef is cool enough to handle, shred with two forks in a large bowl. Set aside.

To prepare the green chili, heat 3 tablespoons of the olive oil in a large, heavy-bottomed Dutch oven or stockpot over medium heat. Add onion and sauté until tender and fragrant, approximately 8 minutes. Add garlic and sauté 2 minutes more. Remove the cooked onion and garlic from the pot and place in the bowl of a food processor fitted with a steel blade. Add the green chiles and parsley and process to a smooth, uniform consistency. Heat the remaining 3 tablespoons of olive oil in the same large heavy-bottomed stockpot over medium heat. Add the flour to the heated oil, stirring constantly in a circular motion. Stir in the cumin, coriander, and oregano to form a smooth paste, working quickly so that the flour does not burn. Carefully stir in the processed chile mixture and beef stock and bring to a boil. Reduce to a simmer and cook to reduce slightly and thicken, approximately 10 minutes. Set aside to cool slightly.

For the burritos:

8 large (approximately 12-inch) flour tortillas

1 bunch radishes, ends removed, thinly sliced

2 tablespoons freshly squeezed lime juice

2 cups shredded Monterey Jack cheese

2 cups cooked pinto beans

1 recipe red chile sauce (page 27)

To assemble your burritos, warm the tortillas on a large comal or in a dry pan, and place on a flat surface. Toss the radish slices with the lime juice in a small bowl. Carefully toss the shredded beef with the cheese and pinto beans. Place approximately 1 cup of the beef mixture in the center of a warmed tortilla and top with several teaspoons of the radish slices. Fold the bottom of the tortilla (the edge closest to you) up and over the filling, then fold each side in and over the bottom. Tightly tuck and roll the burrito away from you to finish. Repeat with remaining tortillas. Top half of each burrito with a generous pour of the red chile sauce and then the other half of each with a generous pour of the green chile sauce. Serve immediately.

YIELD: approximately 8 servings

Thank you, first and foremost, to my two grandmothers, who taught me the value of both cooking with love for people you love and hand-written thank you notes.

A huge and incredibly heartfelt thank you goes out to my blog readers. You all are what make my work possible and you're also what make it so fun. I can't express enough gratitude for bringing me back to my keyboard and comal every single day. Stay hungry!

Thank you so much to Priti Gress, Colette Laroya, Barbara Keane-Pigeon and the whole team at Hippocrene Books. Your guidance, assistance and patience throughout this project are appreciated more than you know. Thank you!

To Yvette Marquez-Sharpnack: you are a creative genius! I am so grateful for the work that you put into making this book look as beautiful as it does. Gracias, mi amiga!

To Stephanie Bridge, thank you so very much for your thoughtful support and for keeping me in line when it comes to PR. Not an easy task, girl - thank you!

Thank you so very much to all my friends and advocates at the Scottsdale Public Library, particularly J.S. and S.S. Keep doing what you do so well every single day - you are so very appreciated.

A big, big shout out to all my friends in the food blogging community, one of the most welcoming groups of which I have ever been lucky enough to be a part. You all are a constant source of inspiration. Plus you make sure I'll never run out of meal ideas. Ever.

Massive thanks and huge hugs to all of my family and friends. We may live far apart, but I love and appreciate all of you so very much. Your encouragement throughout the development of this book and all of my endeavors is so, so valued. Particularly big thanks go out to my dad for all of his well-considered advice: a love of writing (and undying devotion to wienerschnitzel) is clearly in my blood!

Last but not least, thank you to A., my Italian husband and primary taste-tester, who has been sampling enchiladas, tacos and tres leches for over 4 years now. Yes, honey, I will make you chicken parmigiana for dinner tonight.

Love, Meagan AKA Scarletta

index

about the author

Meagan Micozzi was born in New Jersey, raised in Washington, D.C., and educated in New England. When she relocated to the desert of Arizona, she found herself, literally, a fish out of water. Finding comfort and inspiration in the foods of the Southwest, she set out to learn all she could from local chefs and natives and eventually launched Scarletta Bakes, a blog devoted to her original recipes and photography. Her recipes have been featured in *The Huffington Post*, The Kitchn, *Gourmet*, and *Bon Appétit*, and her blog was named a 'Site We Love' by *Saveur*. Micozzi resides in Scottsdale, Arizona. You can visit her at scarlettabakes.com.